CONTENTS

D1196471

042128

EDITOR'S NOTES   1
Arthur M. Cohen

1. All Access Is Not Equal: The Need for Collegiate   3
Education in Community Colleges
Judith S. Eaton
Arguments concerning whether the community college's primary attention
should be, and indeed can be, given to the collegiate function must first be
addressed before a determination can be made of just what a collegiate community college really means in terms of its commitment to access. Strengthening the collegiate function results in stronger access.

2. An Overview of the Total Credit Curriculum   13
Arthur M. Cohen, Jan M. Ignash
The National Curriculum Study conducted by the Center for the Study of
Community Colleges tracked trends in the liberal arts and established a
baseline study of the non–liberal arts community college curriculum.

3. Stability and Change in the Liberal Arts Curriculum   31
Barry VanderKelen
The results of the liberal arts portion of the 1991 National Curriculum Study
are compared to seven previous Center for the Study of Community Colleges curriculum studies spanning sixteen years, revealing remarkable stability in the liberal arts and also substantial changes in a few subject areas.

4. Graduation Requirements,   43
General Education, and the Liberal Arts
Charles R. Brinkman IV
An analysis of forty community colleges indicates that, as a whole, community college general education requirements match their curricular offerings
quite well, assisting in transfer between two-year colleges and between two-
and four-year colleges.

5. Compelling Numbers: English as a Second Language   49
Jan M. Ignash
The results of the National Curriculum Study revealed English as a Second
Language (ESL) to be the fastest-growing area of the curriculum. Commu-
nity colleges may need to evaluate their policies toward the provision of ESL
courses in light of current demographic trends.

6. What Influences Community College   63
Ethnic Studies Course Offerings?
Susan Sean Swayze
While more traditional interdisciplinary ethnic studies course offerings in
community colleges declined in the 1991 National Curriculum Study, re-
sults also reveal that more focused ethnic studies courses, such as "African-
American Writers" or "Asian-American History in the Southwest," appear
to be available.

7. Analyzing Community College Student Transfer Rates   71
Arthur M. Cohen
The development of a consistent, workable definition of student transfer rate
was validated through the results of four Transfer Assembly Projects conducted by the Center for the Study of Community Colleges since 1989.

8. Examining the Relationship Between the Liberal Arts,   81
Course Levels, and Transfer Rates
William B. Armstrong, Melissa Mellissinos
Linking databases containing curriculum and transfer data reveals that colleges with below-average liberal arts ratios have disproportionately low
transfer rates, while colleges above the mean liberal arts ratio tend to have
higher transfer rates.

9. Curriculum and Minority Students   93
Shannon M. Hirose
An exploration of the relationship between curriculum and transfer rates in
colleges with high proportions of minority students suggests that while
minority student transfer rates are not as high as white students', the curriculum does not appear to be an influencing agent.

10. Conclusion: The Future for Curriculum and Transfer   101
Arthur M. Cohen
Over the next few years, economic, demographic, and curricular trends are
likely to bring about an increase in the transfer rate.

INDEX   107

Editor's Notes

The community colleges have long prided themselves on their determination to ensure that everyone, regardless of aspiration, interest, or prior academic attainment, can find courses consonant with their interest. The courses make up the curriculum, the vehicle through which the college expresses its view of what is important for its students to know. Through the curriculum the college's values are revealed.

Periodically the Center for the Study of Community Colleges has tracked the curriculum to see how changes in numbers of courses provided in the different disciplinary areas reflect changing graduation requirements and the rise and fall in popularity of studies in the various fields. Beginning with studies of the humanities in 1975, the center subsequently tabulated the offerings in the sciences, social sciences, fine and performing arts, and, in 1991, the total curriculum, including not only the liberal arts but also the business, technology, trade and industry, health, and other fields that make up the non–liberal arts.

In a parallel effort, since 1989 the center has been tracing the rates at which students transfer from community colleges to baccalaureate-granting institutions, applying a uniform definition and collecting data from a wide array of community colleges and state systems across the nation. These transfer-rate studies continue annually.

The two data sets make it possible to view patterns of curriculum evolution and student flow through the colleges and to associate these two basic dimensions of institutional functioning. The reports in this volume trace the scope of the curriculum, transfer rates, and the relationships between the two.

The volume begins with a chapter by Judith S. Eaton who discusses the liberal arts and occupational curricula, linking them as they reflect college-level studies. She makes a plea for sustaining both areas as a degree-credit, transferable curriculum so that the community colleges can maintain their hard-won position in American higher education.

Chapter Two, by Arthur M. Cohen and Jan M. Ignash, displays the curriculum and enrollments in all the credit-course offerings separated by discipline or field of study. A note on transferability of non–liberal arts courses is included.

The chapter by Barry VanderKelen reports on the magnitude of enrollments in the various disciplines in the liberal arts and shows how with rare exception they have remained consistent for many years.

Charles R. Brinkman's chapter relates the liberal arts curriculum with graduation requirements, indicating how the two reinforce each other.

In Chapter Five, Jan M. Ignash traces the phenomenal rise of English as a Second Language (ESL) that has propelled foreign language study to first place in the humanities and ESL itself to more than half of all class sections in foreign language offerings.

Susan Sean Swayze examines ethnic studies in Chapter Six. Next, in a chapter on calculating transfer rates, Arthur M. Cohen reports how a consistent definition was derived and applied to data retrieved from a sizable proportion of the colleges in the nation. The findings demonstrate that the proportion of students transferring from community colleges to universities has remained stable over several years and that variation in transfer rates between states and between colleges in the same state is quite high.

Chapter Eight, by William B. Armstrong and Melissa Mellissinos, examines the relationship between aspects of the curriculum and transfer rates.

Shannon M. Hirose writes about curriculum patterns in community colleges with high proportions of minority group students, showing how the relationships between student ethnicity and patterns of curriculum offered are not the way the conventional belief would have them.

Arthur Cohen's summary concludes the volume.

Taken together, these chapters reveal that the collegiate function of community colleges is intact. The liberal arts continue to be offered as the basic, lower-division college curriculum. Numerous courses in the non–liberal arts are also used as the introductory curriculum for baccalaureate studies. Sizable numbers of students who begin higher education in community colleges go on to matriculate in four-year colleges and universities. In addition to the community education and direct occupational entry functions of community colleges, their traditional first-two-years-of-college characteristic is still prominent.

Arthur M. Cohen
Editor

ARTHUR M. COHEN is director of the ERIC Clearinghouse for Community Colleges and professor of higher education at the University of California, Los Angeles.

If a community college's primary focus is on the collegiate function, what does this mean in terms of its commitment to access?

All Access Is Not Equal: The Need for Collegiate Education in Community Colleges

Judith S. Eaton

The community college has been the nation's primary site of access to higher education. More students have enrolled in community colleges than in any other individual educational sector. The enormous enrollment growth in the higher education enterprise to which Americans frequently point with pride could not have occurred without the two-year school. Central to occupying this important position has been the community college's investment in its collegiate role: providing the liberal arts and transferable career education that together make up the institution's collegiate function.

Defining Collegiate Education

What is collegiate education and how can it be sustained in an era of conflicting demands? Strong collegiate education in a community college means that its collegiate function is dominant. This occurs when four conditions prevail. First, structured, sequential liberal arts and career education offerings drive the curriculum. They contain the majority of enrollments and offerings. Second, primary attention is given to students' development of college-level competencies through these curricula. These competencies are more important than, for example, "precollege" competencies earned in developmental and remedial

---

This material is based mainly on J. S. Eaton's *Strengthening Collegiate Education in Community Colleges* published by Jossey-Bass in 1994.

programs. Third, the community college environment, through the values faculty and administrators share with students, ensures, to the greatest extent possible, that students are both interested in and prepared for baccalaureate study, whether pursued immediately after community college attendance or at some later point in a student's educational career. Fourth, the community college acknowledges its responsibility as a good citizen of the higher education community; it cooperates with other colleges and universities to ensure that students, if they choose, are able to transfer with ease.

"College-level" competence, a key commitment for the collegiate community college, requires liberal arts or career education that routinely carries associate-degree credit and is transferable for baccalaureate-degree credit. College-level study also requires a level of cognitive complexity that generally characterizes lower-division coursework at most colleges or universities in the country. Cognitive complexity that is adequate for college-level study emerges from intellectual norms that are easily recognizable and accepted in higher education. These norms are embedded in the academic tasks that faculty require students to master. There is not, however, a literature providing more specific definitions of college-level work on which to more precisely anchor the notion of cognitive complexity.

A key test of college-level study is whether or not courses and programs are mobile: whether or not they can be transferred from one institution to another. This test includes not only the familiar two-year to four-year transfer, but also two-year to two-year and four-year to two-year transfer. It is a test of the portability of academic experiences among a variety of higher education institutions. Another test of whether study is college-level is how a two-year institution itself categorizes it: If the study is designated "developmental" or "noncredit" or "not for degree credit" or "training," it is not college-level work. Yet another test is whether or not the four-year institution accepts this study in the form of courses or programs. If a four-year school rejects lower-division coursework from a community college on the basis that it lacks sufficient cognitive complexity (rather than on the basis of whether the four-year institution offers the coursework) the work would not be considered college-level.

Collegiate education as defined here varies from some earlier definitions in that it incorporates a commitment to applied fields (career education) as well as to the major disciplines of the liberal arts. The definition attempts to eliminate the artificial and unworkable distinction between areas of study called "academic" and "career" by applying the criterion "college-level" to both. Academic and career education are bound together by a shared commitment to college-level work.

As described here, collegiate education identifies the community college as firmly within higher education. Collegiate community colleges are not extensions of high school, nor one of many quasi-educational services offered by a community. The dominance of the collegiate function makes college-level

studies the foundation of all academic decision making. It is the core commitment that should set the agenda of the national leadership of the community
college enterprise.

When the collegiate function is dominant within the community college,
it defines and structures comprehensiveness. Collegiate community colleges
can undertake some of the other programs and services that are identified with
comprehensiveness provided that these are built upon a collegiate foundation.
For example, a dominant collegiate function does not preclude terminal vocational education that is not college-level, but this should not dominate the curriculum. The collegiate function does not preclude the community-based
function of the community college, but attention to community-based services
should not be its dominant activity.

Many objections have been raised in the past to efforts ensuring that the
community college is a collegiate institution. The objections center around the
notion that a collegiate community college—as compared to other community
colleges—somehow limits the scope of service of the two-year institution: A
collegiate community college would diminish responsiveness and comprehensiveness, contribute to educational elitism, and destroy educational opportunity. These objections have been effectively used to constrict collegiate
education in the community college.

In addition to these objections, many long-standing features of community college life work against its collegiate success. The tolerance of idiosyn-
cratic student attendance patterns, the influence of narrowly focused vocational
and demand-driven visions of the community college, the pressure of underprepared students, ongoing public misunderstanding of the educational role
of the community college, and the prejudice of community college educators
themselves toward functioning as part of the higher education enterprise can—
and do—coalesce to reduce the collegiate commitment of the community college. These features, coupled with ongoing indifference from community
college leaders, might even be sufficient, in the long run, to eliminate this interpretation of the community college mission.

Should the Community College Be Collegiate?

There are strong educational, social, and economic arguments on which
to maintain "yes, the community college should be collegiate." To argue that the
community college should be collegiate is to make a decision about what
the community college ought to do—what is right for students and society. It
is a public policy judgement that has strong social and moral overtones.

Educationally, the collegiate function is the community college's most powerful expression of its commitment to access. The collegiate function enhances
the educational value of access in dramatic ways. Students in liberal arts or
career education programs that are college-level have the greatest actual and

potential educational gains of any group of students in the community college. There is a clear, documentable relationship between collegiate study and educational attainment.

Economically, the collegiate community college provides a greater return on investment for both students and taxpayers. Students in college-level courses and programs receive more academically challenging education than students in other community college programs. This, in turn, provides them with enhanced mobility, enabling them to pursue either the baccalaureate or more demanding jobs or both. It is the pathway to enhance occupational status and increase earnings. Taxpayers, at present, invest less per student in community colleges than most other forms of public higher education. For this, they have enjoyed a rich return: Millions of students for whom higher education had not been economically feasible now attend college. This investment does carry some risks, however. While taxpayer investment in the community college is sound for some, it has a negative side for others. Many underprepared students attend community colleges and, as some critics have pointed out, taxpayers are supporting some students who are academically marginal and perhaps do not belong in college at all.

Socially, the community college is a pivotal educational institution for dealing with low-income students, individuals experiencing change in life circumstances, and especially minority students. The community college is at the front line of educational efforts to deal with racism, poverty, and undereducation. For disadvantaged groups served by the community college, its collegiate experience is the richest educational opportunity they can have. Given the reliance of some minorities on the community college, the collegiate function is central to assisting them to end economic and social disparity based on race, especially through enabling minorities to gain access to the baccalaureate.

The collegiate community college is an extraordinary educational response in a democratic society to providing the best of higher education to as many people as can reasonably benefit. It is a profound statement of this country's unique valuing of the individual and its faith in its future. As a collegiate institution, the community college is central to providing, sustaining, and expanding educational opportunity and accomplishment in society.

Can the Community College Be Collegiate?

Based on its history and its resources, especially its faculty, the community college has a strong collegiate capacity. Examination of the history of the educational role of the community college indicates that the collegiate function has consistently been a part of the two-year college. The liberal arts/transfer function was key to the establishment of the early junior college. Whether measured by the commitment of its leadership, course and program offerings, or student enrollments, there is evidence that a good number of two-year colleges met the four conditions required to be collegiate institutions: A majority of enrollments and offerings were in structured, sequential liberal arts and career education; the offerings were at an appropriate level of cognitive complexity; students' pursuit of longer-range educational goals was an important value in the institution; and students transferred with ease.

The collegiate community college has the benefit of significant internal resources. Financially, although support for community colleges on a per full-time-equivalent (FTE) basis is not as great as it should be, it does cover the actual cost of instruction in many college-level courses and programs. Another essential resource is the community college faculty, the majority of whom have solid backgrounds in college-level study and retain a strong interest in the collegiate function. They are experienced, talented teachers who have met the most demanding challenges in American higher education. They have taken on classrooms where student skills vary dramatically and responded with creative approaches to teaching and curriculum. Surveys consistently confirm their interest in the collegiate work of the community college. The community college curricula, whether liberal arts or career education, are, for the most part, considered college-level. More than three-quarters of community colleges have a transfer function.

Externally, building a dominant collegiate function is encouraged by the great national need for more challenging education, a better-informed citizenry, and a workforce with flexible skills and an ability for independent thinking. Social equity concerns alone are a powerful incentive for a collegiate community college. Community colleges remain the single most important resource for economic and social gain through education. Establishing a dominant collegiate function is a valuable response to public policy initiatives that address education equity and the social justice needs of the society.

Sustaining a collegiate capacity has not been without challenge, however. Alternative visions of the community college such as those that stress its role as a terminal degree institution have limited the full expression of the collegiate role. The collegiate role of the community college has had serious competition over the years. The transition from "junior" to "community" college had a particularly negative impact on the collegiate function: Other community college purposes such as terminal occupational education, developmental and remedial education, and community services grew dramatically and the collegiate function diminished in scope and importance.

Although there is a significant historical function for the collegiate role, it has not enjoyed strong support from the official national leadership of the community college. Since 1959, that leadership has not placed priority on the collegiate function. For more than 30 years, the collegiate function has received at best perfunctory support. As a result, when federal legislation, state legislation, and public policy focused on the community college, attention was concentrated on other purposes—especially terminal occupational education.

Externally, many four-year college educators and many education writers do not believe that the community college is—or can be—a collegiate institution. (See for example, Brint and Karabel, 1989, and Astin, 1993.) They perceive the community college to be devoted solely to terminal vocational education, training, or developmental education. They view it as valuable only to provide skills for lower-wage, lower-status jobs. However well intentioned, these individuals contribute to a vision of the community college as a subcollegiate institution.

In spite of the competition and the limited leadership commitment, the collegiate function has remained important in the community college. This is due to its vitality and the need that it meets. Given the survival of the collegiate function under these rather negative conditions, it is reasonable to be optimistic about establishing the collegiate function as dominant.

What Will a Collegiate Community College Mean?

There are serious implications associated with the advocacy of a dominant collegiate function in the community college. Some may view these implications as reasons for firmly establishing the collegiate function. Others may view them as early warnings about the difficulty of sustaining a dominant collegiate function. Yet others will see the implications as serious obstacles for a dominant collegiate function and might choose to reject the collegiate emphasis as central to community college efforts.

A collegiate community college is a choice among the three major visions of the contemporary community college. There have been three compelling yet quite different perceptions of the community college's primary role: the community-based model as developed by Edmund Gleazer, president of the American Association of Junior Colleges (later the American Association of Community and Junior Colleges) 1959–1979 (Gleazer 1980); the terminal occupational education model as developed by Dale Parnell, president of the American Association of Community and Junior Colleges 1979–1991 (Hull and Parnell 1991; Parnell 1984); and the collegiate-comprehensiveness model as developed by Arthur Cohen and Florence Brawer at the University of California, Los Angeles (Cohen and Brawer, 1987). The Cohen/Brawer model is the only vision on which it makes sense to develop a collegiate community college.

Building a collegiate community college redefines intellectual opportunity. For students in the community college, the vision of intellectual opportunity cannot be confined to only the community college experience. The vision must expand to incorporate students, at some point in their lives, moving on to other levels of education, especially the baccalaureate.

A collegiate community college diminishes mission ambiguity. The educational role of the community college has always been equivocal. A collegiate community college resolves this ambiguity of place and role. The community college is part of higher education, and thus its primary commitment is to college-level work. Its other programs and services are developed in the context of being a higher education institution and the commitment to college-level work.

A collegiate community college restricts the commitment to access. This is not a choice between open access and restricted access. The community college has always been a limited access institution—but with fewer restrictions than other institutions that call themselves "open access" or "nonselective." With a dominant collegiate function, the community college access commitment becomes even more restricted. Students must be prepared for college-level work and have, at most, modest remediation needs in order to enroll in most courses and programs. This is an expansion of the existing practice of limiting enrollments in some courses and programs based on student demonstration of skill levels needed for these undertakings. Students in need of serious remediation will need to attend other education sites that can assist them in developing the skills needed for college-level work.

A collegiate community college requires vigorous leadership in the development of effective college-preparatory experiences outside the community college. Establishing a dominant collegiate function means that the community college diminishes its responsibility for developmental and remedial education. Other educational sites and, in the long run, improved elementary and secondary schools, must take primary responsibility for producing college-ready students. The community college alone cannot function as the full answer to democratic education in society. It takes the effective functioning of all levels of education to achieve this goal.

A collegiate community college requires additional attention to relationships with other levels of education. The community college is positioned squarely within higher education. This increases the need for coordination with four-year colleges and universities, especially in relation to transfer efforts. It also increases the reliance on elementary and secondary education because of the collegiate function's requirement that students be ready or close-to-ready for college-level work.

A collegiate community college makes additional demands on the nontraditional role of these institutions. Community colleges will function as sites of nontraditional delivery of collegiate education in a nontraditional setting. The higher education community—including the community college—has for too long assumed that students being "nontraditional" means that they cannot avail themselves of a collegiate education—the disciplines, the intellectual challenge of advanced work, the benefits of scholarship. This assumption is false and community colleges can take the lead in building models of collegiate education provided in nontraditional ways.

A collegiate community college accepts—and gains strength from—some of the advice of its critics. Stated in the most positive light, the community college critics are urging that the community colleges become serious academic institutions devoted to college-level work: sequential, structured educational experiences that will, at some point, assist a large number of students in succeeding at a baccalaureate level. The critics seek this goal because they believe that the educational, economic, and social gains at the baccalaureate level far exceed these gains at the associate degree level.

A collegiate community college calls for reconsideration of the associate degree. The associate degree is a weak credential in the community college. It is not clear whether or not it makes a difference in students' educational gains. Yet, the degree is consistently used by many community colleges to structure curriculum and make other important academic decisions, even if students can ignore their impact. Structured, sequential educational experiences *are* needed. If the associate degree is not an effective strategy to meet this need, others should be developed.

A collegiate community college is an extraordinary opportunity for faculty. It can revitalize faculty commitment to teaching and learning and build an agenda for applied research and scholarship. A dominant collegiate function can place faculty in a national leadership role in shaping and defining undergraduate education. It can help community college faculty create an intellectual community and establish the community college as a serious academic institution.

Summary

All access is not equal. Access to collegiate education is a stronger and more powerful form of educational opportunity because of the skills it can provide and the potential for educational and other gains for students. The decision to strengthen collegiate education, however, is difficult and controversial. This is because it demands skill levels of students that contradict the community college investment in education for anyone who wants to try. It calls for structured education and this is in conflict with the freedom of choice long familiar to students as they make decisions about curriculum. It demands that students demonstrate college-level competencies and that institutions refuse to tolerate subcollegiate work—challenging the more comfortable approach that student achievement at any level, collegiate or subcollegiate, is considered "success."

Yet, the commitment to collegiate education is the community college's most compelling message that it truly seeks to function as "democracy's college." Community college leaders make a rich and rewarding contribution to the future through their efforts to strengthen the collegiate role.

References

Astin, A. W. *What Matters in College?* San Francisco: Jossey-Bass, 1993.

Brint, S., and Karabel, J. *The Diverted Dream: Community Colleges and the Promise of Educational Opportunity in America, 1900–1985.* New York: Oxford University Press, 1989.

Cohen, A. M., and Brawer, F. B. *The Collegiate Function of the Community Colleges: Fostering Higher Learning Through Curriculum and Student Transfer.* San Francisco: Jossey-Bass, 1987.

Gleazer, E. J., Jr. *The Community College: Values, Vision, and Vitality.* Washington, D.C.: American Association of Community and Junior Colleges, 1980.

Hull, D., and Parnell, D. (comps.). *Tech-Prep Associate Degree: A Win/Win Experience.* Waco, Tex.: Center for Occupational Research and Development, Inc., 1991.

Parnell, D. *2 + 2 Tech Prep/Associate Degree Program: A Working Degree For America: A Concept Paper.* Washington, D.C.: American Association of Community and Junior Colleges, 1984.

JUDITH S. EATON is president of the Council for Aid to Education in New York City. Prior to her appointment to the council, she was vice president at the American Council on Education in Washington, D.C.

How much of the total community college curriculum is devoted to the liberal arts? What are the "non–liberal arts" and how much of the community college curriculum is devoted to each of the non–liberal arts? How much of the non–liberal arts curriculum is transferable to four-year colleges?

An Overview of the Total Credit Curriculum

Arthur M. Cohen, Jan M. Ignash

The liberal arts as a focus of study derive from the belief that human knowledge and societal cohesion are grounded in rationality. In the earliest American colleges, this doctrine gave rise to a curriculum centering on philosophy, languages, science, and rhetoric. Subsequently, the liberal arts were codified in academic disciplines in the universities and expanded as new ways of organizing knowledge came to the fore. When the community colleges were founded early in the twentieth century they installed the liberal arts, gradually modifying them in accordance with shifting fashions of academic organization and with attention to the capabilities and interests of their students. Despite frequent attempts to shift the curriculum toward studies more directly vocational, the liberal arts, with over half the enrollment, remain the centerpiece of community college studies.

The Center for the Study of Community Colleges (CSCC) has examined the liberal arts in community colleges nationwide in a series of studies that began with a grant from the National Endowment for the Humanities in 1975. In 1992, for the first time in the sixteen years the CSCC has been studying the community college curriculum, the center tracked the credit courses outside the liberal arts. This non–liberal arts portion of the curriculum, accounting for only one-fourth or less of the total community college curriculum well into the 1950s, now accounts for 43 percent of the total credit curriculum. In addition, numerous courses in this segment of the curriculum, once considered "terminal" education designed to lead directly to employment, now can be transferred for baccalaureate credit. Clearly, the non–liberal arts have grown in terms of proportion of the curriculum offered and as an avenue to further study. The second half of this chapter reports the results of the non–liberal arts study conducted by the CSCC.

The Liberal Arts

The data for the liberal arts study were obtained from 164 community colleges throughout the United States by randomly sampling the colleges listed in the 1990 *Directory of the American Association of Community and Junior Colleges.* The sample was approximately balanced according to size with fifty-one small (less than 1,500 students), fifty-six medium, and fifty-seven large (over 6,000 students) colleges in the set. Because a special effort was made to include the colleges that were participating in the National Center for Academic Achievement and Transfer's partnership grant program, the sample was tilted somewhat toward colleges that enroll higher proportions of underrepresented minority-group students.

Catalogs and class schedules for spring 1991 were obtained from the colleges, and course sections in the liberal arts were counted and tallied according to the coding scheme used in the prior studies. The scheme divides the liberal arts curriculum into six major disciplines—humanities, English, fine and performing arts, social sciences, sciences, and mathematics and computer sciences. These six disciplines are further divided into fifty-five broad subject areas, with these in turn further divided into 245 sub-subject areas. For example, the sub-subject area "French" is part of the broad subject area "foreign languages," which is part of the "humanities" discipline. For a course section to be listed, the class schedule had to designate a meeting time and place; laboratory, independent study, cooperative, apprenticeship, and field work classes were not included.

To code each liberal arts course at the appropriate level of proficiency, definitions for remedial, standard, and advanced courses were used. *Remedial* applies to any compensatory, developmental, or basic course that is below college-level proficiency and which typically does not carry college transfer credit. *Standard* courses are "first-tier" or "introductory" courses that have no same-subject-area prerequisite for enrollment and carry college graduation or transfer credit. *Advanced* courses carry a prerequisite in the same or a related field as a condition for enrollment.

After coding and tallying the liberal arts classes into the appropriate sub-subject areas, a random sample of every tenth section under each broad subject area was pulled. The colleges were asked to provide either second-census or end-of-the-term enrollment figures for this sample. The number of sections that had been canceled in each subject area was also noted. Enrollment and average class size figures were then calculated, based on the 164 colleges, and extrapolated to the population of 1,250 U.S. community colleges. Finally, the scheduled course sections in the remainder of the curriculum were counted in order to determine an approximate ratio of liberal arts to non–liberal arts offerings.

In general, the liberal arts have expanded. In 1991 they accounted for around 56 percent of the curriculum, up from 52 percent in 1986. Very little of this expansion can be traced to innovation or new course designs; most resulted from higher proportions of the students enrolling in traditional liberal arts classes.

With few exceptions the liberal arts reveal remarkable stability. Many of the subject areas continue to be offered in nearly all (90 percent plus) of the colleges: history, literature, political science, English, economics, psychology, sociology, biology, chemistry, math, and computer science. Total enrollments in these subjects reflect their dominance (Table 2.1). However, the ubiquity of the offerings and the enrollment figures mask certain changes.

Foreign languages are offered in less than 90 percent of the colleges but their enrollments, tripling between 1978 and 1991, are exceeded only by English and math. In that same thirteen-year interval, enrollments in psychology, biology, physics, chemistry, and math doubled, but those in literature, history, and political science changed hardly at all. Therefore, although some basic subjects continue to be offered nearly everywhere, the overall number of students taking them has shifted markedly. Nearly all the increase in foreign language enrollment was in English as a Second Language, detailed in Chapter Five.

Other changes were seen in special-group and remedial studies. The CSCC staff coded such courses as women's literature, African-American history, and sociology of Mexican Americans in group literature (offered in more than half of the colleges), history of special groups (more than one-third of the colleges), and sociology of particular groups (found in one-fourth of the colleges), respectively. Ethnic studies, coded only if it was listed as a separate course or program, was found in only 10 percent of the colleges. Thus the CSCC findings should not be compared with those reported by Levine and Curreton (1992), who tallied each special-group course as ethnic studies or women's studies.

Remedial studies continue their prominence in English and math (Tables 2.2 and 2.3). Around 30 percent of the class sections offered in English are at the remedial level, down from 37 percent fifteen years ago, and the percentage of remedial math classes dropped in half, from 32 to 16 percent. These changes resulted not because the incoming students were better prepared but because math labs have become more widespread and the CSCC study did not count enrollments in lab courses. Furthermore, much of the remedial English instruction is taking place in tutorial settings and in courses coded as college-level introductory composition but which may be taken repeatedly; Florida's College Level Academic Skills Test requirement, for example, has stimulated much of the latter.

Intracourse shifts undoubtedly have been occurring as well. Certainly few, if any, instructors are teaching U.S. history to 1877 in the same fashion as they were; the texts and syllabi have been modified to account for the contributions

Table 2.1. Total Student Enrollment (Duplicated Head Count) and Average Class Size for All Liberal Arts Areas

	Enrollment	Average Class Size
Humanities		
Art history/appreciation	84,700	28
Cultural anthropology	31,100	30
Foreign languages	460,700	20
History	396,500	31
Interdisciplinary humanities (includes cultural geography)	94,200	35
Literature	120,900	23
Fine and performing arts history/appreciation	29,900	28
Music history/appreciation	65,600	27
Philosophy and logic	143,200	29
Political science	249,000	29
Religious studies	14,300	35
Social/ethnic studies	13,400	26
English	1,317,400	21
Fine and Performing Arts		
Dance	27,600	16
Music	95,800	11
Theater	19,600	14
Visual arts	151,700	11
Social Sciences		
Anthropology	28,000	23
Economics	173,500	27
Geography	19,500	24
Interdisciplinary social sciences	30,100	20
Psychology	455,100	30
Sociology	256,300	31
Sciences		
Biological sciences (includes agricultural science/natural resources)	409,300	26
Chemistry	130,200	20
Earth and space sciences (includes environmental science)	85,100	32
Engineering sciences and technology	102,200	15
Geology	24,100	24
Integrated science	43,400	27
Physics	80,100	19
Mathematics and Computer Sciences		
Introductory and intermediate mathematics	766,100	24
Advanced mathematics	87,700	20
Applied math/technology-related	41,600	18
Computer science	147,200	23
Math for other majors	99,700	23
Statistics and probability	69,000	27

Table 2.2. Percentage of Colleges Providing Remedial, Standard,
and Advanced Courses in the Six Major Discipline Areas

Discipline	Remedial	Standard	Advanced
Humanities	1%	97%	80%
English	89	99	84
Fine and performing arts	0	83	75
Social science	0	98	59
Science	5	100	87
Math and computer science	65	98	86

Table 2.3. Percentage of Remedial, Standard, and Advanced
Course Offerings in Each Major Discipline Area

Discipline	Remedial	Standard	Advanced
Humanities	0.1%	82.5%	17.4%
English	30.5	49.7	19.8
Fine and performing arts	0.0	62.8	37.2
Social science	0.0	85.8	14.2
Science	1.0	67.6	31.7
Math and computer science	15.9[a]	62.2	21.9

[a]Self-paced, individualized, and lab courses were not counted. A large number of remedial math courses were self-paced, individualized, and lab courses; this would explain the low remedial math percentage.

of women and minorities. But if the course carries the same title it is coded as the same course.

A perennial problem in comparing rural colleges with urban colleges, and small colleges with large colleges, is that few rural colleges are large and few urban colleges are small; therefore, any differences that appear may be related to size or to locale, or to both. The distribution of colleges in the CSCC sample points to the pattern: only three of the small colleges were in urban settings and only two of the large colleges were in rural areas.

College size is only modestly related to general curriculum patterns. With the exception of a tilt toward science in the smaller colleges and humanities in the larger ones (an effect of the numerous sections of English as a Second Language), rounding error may account for the small differences found. However, the curriculum in the medium-sized rural colleges includes a smaller percentage of remedial courses and a larger percentage of advanced courses. The rural institutions offer three sections of advanced courses for every remedial section offered, while suburban institutions offer 1.9 and urban institutions offer 1.4 advanced sections for every remedial section. For the overall sample, the ratio is 2.2 advanced sections for each remedial section. These differences are more pronounced than those based on size, and suggest some real differences in the structure of the curriculum. As has been argued by Richardson and Bender (1985), urban institutions apparently *do* devote a greater proportion of their curriculum to remedial studies, and, consequently, a smaller proportion to advanced level courses.

The availability of specialized courses in certain disciplines varies even more markedly. The smaller institutions cannot offer as many total class sections as the medium and larger ones. What choices do they make? Table 2.4 displays the subject areas provided. The larger the college, the greater the likelihood of its offering courses other than the basic general studies requirements. From art history to statistics the ratio of colleges providing the specialized classes drops as college size decreases, with the most pronounced differences coming in cultural anthropology, cultural geography, dance, earth/space science, fine arts appreciation, and geology. Differences of this magnitude do not show up in comparing the medium-sized colleges on the basis of location.

In summary, the major liberal arts disciplines are evenly distributed across all community colleges regardless of size or setting, suggesting that students seeking a general education can obtain the basic courses anywhere. Finding advanced courses and courses in specialized subject areas is a different matter. Students at large community colleges have a wide variety of subjects to choose from, but students at smaller colleges and those in rural areas may find fewer choices.

The Non–Liberal Arts

That the non–liberal arts have flourished in recent years is due to a variety of factors. As the CSCC non–liberal arts study will show, a high percentage of non–liberal arts courses in many subject areas are directly transferable to four-year institutions. This factor may be paramount in underscoring the "validity" of the non–liberal arts, since students are not foreclosing their options for further studies through the pursuit of study of the non–liberal arts. A second factor is that of prestige. As many professions require increased years of study as a condition for employment, the status of those professions rises accordingly. Non–liberal arts education need not therefore be viewed as education leading away from a baccalaureate degree.

Methodology. Two major objectives drove the non–liberal arts study. The first was to quantify the proportion of the curriculum devoted to the non–liberal arts and the second was to discover the percentage of non–liberal arts courses that are transferable to four-year institutions. Because the non–liberal arts study was the first of its kind conducted by the CSCC, a taxonomy had to be developed. Based largely on the "Taxonomy of Academic and Vocational Courses for Less-than-4-Year Postsecondary Institutions" (Grubb, 1987), a CSCC taxonomy was developed for the non–liberal arts courses using ten

Table 2.4. Percentage of Community Colleges Offering Liberal Arts Classes, by Institutional Size

	Large	Medium	Small	All Colleges
Humanities				
Art history/appreciation	57%	88%	91%	81%
Cultural anthropology	15	37	83	47
Cultural geography	6	24	40	24
Foreign languages	70	88	98	87
History	83	92	93	92
Interdisciplinary humanities	26	42	71	48
Literature	81	93	98	92
Fine and performing arts history/appreciation	19	41	74	46
Music history/appreciation	51	71	86	71
Philosophy and logic	55	68	95	79
Political science	83	86	98	90
Religious studies	13	25	26	22
Social/ethnic studies	8	3	31	15
English	98	98	100	99
Fine and Performing Arts				
Dance	6	24	40	24
Music	42	73	90	70
Theater	26	51	60	47
Visual arts	57	86	97	82
Social Sciences				
Anthropology	17	22	29	34
Economics	87	93	98	93
Geography	28	42	57	43
History/sociology/philosophy of science	2	5	7	5
Interdisciplinary social sciences	21	32	50	35
Psychology	96	98	100	98
Sociology	83	97	100	94
Sciences				
Agriculture and natural resources	17	17	19	18
Biological sciences	83	97	100	95
Chemistry	79	97	100	93
Earth/space science	19	44	81	50
Engineering	45	80	97	76
Environmental science	15	10	26	17
Geology	21	33	69	43
Integrated science	34	41	62	46
Physics	74	86	98	87
Mathematics and Computer Sciences				
Introductory and intermediate mathematics	96	98	100	98
Advanced mathematics	68	88	98	86
Applied math/technology-related	38	56	72	57
Computer science	77	92	98	89
Math for other majors	62	85	93	81
Statistics and probability	50	83	98	79

major discipline areas: agriculture technology, business and office, marketing, health, home economics, technical education, engineering technology, trade and industry, education, and other.

The major categories and specific course areas for the non–liberal arts are as follows:

Agriculture
Horticulture, agribusiness and crop production, forest products and other agriculture products, agricultural sciences, renewable natural resources, animal health technology, nursery operation

Business and Office
Accounting, taxes, business and management, secretarial and related (filing, typing, shorthand, 10-key calculations), labor law, will, trusts and estate planning, legal assistant, other business and office, airline ticketing and reservations

Marketing and Distribution
Real estate, fashion merchandising, salesmanship, auctioneering, advertising design layout, purchasing textiles

Health
Nursing, health sciences, allied health, cardiopulmonary resuscitation, emergency technician, nutrition, marriage and family counseling courses, drug counseling, working with juvenile delinquents, dental assisting, corrective and rehabilitative physical education or other physical therapy for the physically challenged

Home Economics
Home economics, sewing, cooking, preserving foods, home interior decorating, all home economics courses not focused on trade and industry and intended for one's personal use at home

Technical Education
Computer software applications (word processing, spreadsheets, database programs, networking, desktop publishing—all nonprogramming computer applications); protective services (fire, police and law enforcement, lifeguard, military science courses); communication technologies (journalism, TV, newspaper reporting, radio announcing, photojournalism and other mass media courses, graphics, offset printing); commercial photography

Engineering Technologies
Most of this category was coded under the spring 1991 liberal arts study. Engineering courses that were too occupationally oriented to be coded in the lib-

eral arts, however, were coded under non–liberal arts. These non–liberal arts engineering courses focus on engineering principles such as "analog or digital fundamentals" or "AC/DC current" or "Ohm's law" as well as more practical subject matter. Examples: "avionics" (theory of flight and practical aspects of flying an airplane) or "industrial electricity."

Trade and Industry
Construction; automotive; aviation engineering (concerning the manufacture of airplanes); surveying; drafting, including CAD/CAM; other mechanics and repairers; welding and precision metal; other precision production; transport and materials moving; consumer/personal/miscellaneous services, including cosmetology, upholstery; hospitality industry courses, including culinary arts and wines; pattern design and many apparel construction courses; travel and tourist agent

Personal Skills and Avocational Courses
Physical education, freshman orientation, introduction to the library, parenting, fashion color analysis, career and life planning, self-appraisal courses

Education
Early childhood education, physical education instructor courses, coaching, children's literature, nanny courses, math or music or art for teachers, courses for future instructors of the emotionally and mentally challenged

Other
Social services program training courses, library cataloguing procedures.

How Much of the Community College Curriculum Is Occupied by the Non–Liberal Arts? The non–liberal arts study revealed that slightly more than 80 percent of the for-credit non–liberal arts curriculum was occupied by just four discipline areas: business and office, personal skills and avocational courses, trade and industry, and technical education (Table 2.5). Physical education accounted for over 90 percent of the courses coded under Personal Skills, and computer software applications was the largest category of courses coded under Technical Education.

Five discipline areas accounted for only a small portion of the non–liberal arts credit curriculum, altogether accounting for just under 10 percent. Few courses were coded in the areas of agriculture (1.2 percent), marketing and distribution (3.4 percent), home economics (0.2 percent), engineering technology (0.2 percent), or education (2.5 percent). Several of these categories bear explanation.

For agriculture and engineering categories, courses were coded under liberal arts as well as non–liberal arts. Courses that were more theoretically based and less oriented toward a specific occupation were considered liberal arts

Table 2.5. Number of Sections and Percentage of Non–Liberal Arts Courses Offered

Discipline	Number of Course Sections Offered	Percentage of Non–Liberal Arts Sections	Percentage of Total Credit Sections
Business and office	11,156	24.6%	10.7%
Personal skills and avocational courses	8,643	19.1	8.3
Trade and industry	8,420	18.6	8.1
Technical education	8,229	18.1	7.9
Health	4,641	10.2	4.4
Marketing and distribution	1,523	3.4	1.5
Education	1,147	2.5	1.1
Engineering technologies	889	2.0	.9
Agriculture	529	1.2	.5
Home economics	106	.2	.1
Other	77	.2	.1
Total	45,360	100.0%	43.4%

courses. Both agriculture and engineering declined between 1986 and 1991, the former probably because of sampling error in a field that accounts for a minuscule proportion of the curriculum, the latter because courses such as graphics may have been counted as visual arts and CAD/CAM as technical education.

Other gray areas include home economics and education. Very few "true" home economics courses were found; only courses in baking, cooking, and sewing for one's personal use *at home* were included. Classes such as pattern design, fabrics, wines, culinary arts, and refrigeration for restaurants were often clearly trade and industry classes, as judged by both course titles and course descriptions. Using this taxonomy, then, the category "home economics" all but disappeared, accounting for only 0.2 percent of the non–liberal arts curriculum. The great majority of classes coded under education were early childhood education courses, and a few were fitness instructor training courses. Lower-division education has become a rarity as the academic major and the fifth college year or master's degree have become the dominant requirements for neophyte teachers.

What Is the Ratio of Liberal Arts to Non–Liberal Arts? For the spring 1991 National Liberal Arts Curriculum Study, 59,205 liberal arts course sections were tallied by staff at the CSCC, while in the parallel study of the non–liberal arts, 45,360 sections were tallied, for a total of 104,565 course sections coded in the two studies. A 56.5 percent to 43.4 percent ratio of liberal arts to non–liberal arts courses resulted.

Table 2.6 presents the percentage breakdown of the total curriculum by major subject area, providing a description of the percentages occupied by the

Table 2.6. Percentage of Total Curriculum by Major Discipline Areas

Discipline	Number of Sections	Percentage of Total Curriculum
Humanities	14,034	13.42%
English	13,327	12.75
Math and computer sciences	11,176	10.69
Business and office	11,156	10.67
Personal skills and avocational courses	8,643	8.27
Trade and industry	8,420	8.05
Technical education	8,229	7.87
Sciences	8,031	7.68
Social sciences	6,966	6.66
Fine and performing arts	5,671	5.42
Health	4,641	4.44
Marketing	1,523	1.46
Education	1,147	1.10
Engineering technologies	889	0.85
Agriculture (non–liberal arts)	529	0.51
Home economics	106	0.10
Other	77	0.07
Total	104,565	100.0%

six liberal arts and ten non–liberal arts discipline areas that make up the total credit curriculum.

How Much of the Non–Liberal Arts Transfer? As a second component of the non–liberal arts study, course transferability rates[1] were calculated for the states of California, Illinois, and Texas. Because any course at a community college is likely to be accepted for transfer credit by some four-year institution somewhere within the state, transferability rates were calculated from community colleges to two specific types of four-year institutions—a "flagship" research university and a comprehensive college or university.[2]

In order to create a uniform basis of comparison between states, "transferability" was defined as course-to-course transfer equivalencies rather than "program" or "block" transferability of courses between institutions. Transferable courses were those that carried credit to four-year institutions in one of four categories: general education credit, general elective credit, specific course credit in a major field, or major field elective credit. The goal was to discover which courses a student could count on transferring to four-year institutions—even if that student had taken only a few community college courses.

Because the method of determining transferability of courses differs between states, a generic methodology for collecting these data for the three states involved in the study was not possible. In California, course transferability was recorded right in the college course schedules; in Texas, articulation officers at the community colleges provided the data; and in Illinois, transfer guides were obtained from the state postsecondary agency and used to calculate percentages of courses in each of the ten major non–liberal arts areas that transfer to four-year institutions. The results are presented below for the states of California, Texas, and Illinois.

What Transfers in the Non–Liberal Arts in California? The system for assessing course transferability in California is fairly simple. State mandate obliges community colleges to list in their catalogs or schedules which courses will transfer to one of the two public systems of higher education in the state— the University of California (UC) system, with nine campuses, or the California State University (CSU) system, with twenty campuses. Some community college schedules and catalogs list which individual campuses within the entire system will accept a specific course for transfer credit, whereas others merely list a course as acceptable for transfer somewhere with the UC or CSU systems. Determining transferability, therefore, was easy because catalogs and schedules clearly designated individual course transferability.

Thirty California community colleges participated in this phase of the non–liberal arts study. Not surprisingly, the findings for California indicated very different transferability rates from the community colleges to the research universities of the UC system and to the state comprehensive universities, the CSU system. Within the UC system, only courses within the area of personal skills and avocational courses transferred in high numbers (76.7 percent), largely because of the extremely high percentage of physical education courses that transferred. In fact, the personal skills subject area accounted for 26.5 percent of the non–liberal arts curriculum for California, a full 7.4 percentage points higher than the national percentage of 19.1 percent (Table 2.7).

Table 2.7. Transferability of California Non–Liberal Arts Courses

Transfer Subject Area	CSU	UC
Agriculture	64.5%	21.0%
Business and office	61.0	23.0
Marketing and distribution	70.3	1.6
Health	54.3	16.3
Home economics	47.1	12.9
Technical education	52.8	11.0
Engineering technology	62.6	5.7
Trade and industry	35.7	3.7
Personal skills and avocational courses	88.0	76.7
Education	70.6	5.6
Other	94.1	35.3
Overall Transferability	61.7%	28.9%

Note: N = 30.

Within the state comprehensive university system, however, an overall 61.7 percent of community colleges courses transferred, with a range of from 88 percent in personal skills courses to a low of 35.7 percent in trade and industry courses. In both the UC and CSU systems, trade and industry courses held among the lowest rankings in percentage of transferable courses. If trade and industry courses were the only non–liberal arts courses considered, then some merit might exist in the charge that students who take non–liberal arts courses are denied access to four-year degrees via the transfer function. But taken as a whole, the non–liberal arts show remarkable transferability to the state university system and challenge the notion that students who take courses in these fields are "cooled out" of baccalaureate degree programs. Some worth may exist, however, in the proposition that a status difference does exist among the various subjects of the non–liberal arts. Certainly, for students who are enrolled in trade and industry programs, baccalaureate degrees appear less accessible.

What Transfers in Texas? Eleven Texas community colleges participated in the transferability component of the non–liberal arts study. Transfer articulation coordinators at these colleges provided written transfer agreements designating courses as transferable or nontransferable to the flagship research institution in Texas, the University of Texas at Austin, and to one of two state comprehensive universities, Stephen F. Austin State or Southwest Texas State. Table 2.8 provides the results for Texas.

The results for Texas are surprising in that the overall transferability rate, as well as rates for a number of individual subject areas, are quite close. A mere 5.3 percentage points differentiate overall transferability rates between the state's flagship research institution and two state comprehensive universities. This pattern is quite different from that of California.

Table 2.8. Transferability of Texas Non–Liberal Arts Courses

Transfer Subject Area	State Comprehensive University	Research University
Agriculture	28.0%	16.0%
Business and office	41.0	30.3
Marketing and distribution	43.9	39.4
Health	7.4	6.8
Home economics	N.A.[a]	N.A.
Technical education	71.1	56.2
Engineering technology	0	0
Trade and industry	5.8	5.8
Personal skills and avocational courses	100.0	99.8
Education	50.0	17.4
Other	N.A.	N.A.
Overall Transferability	41.6%	35.3%

Note: N = 11.

[a] Too few selections were coded to provide reliable data.

Further study of transferability in Texas yielded an interesting case study in which data were obtained on transferability percentages of one community college to fifteen different four-year institutions in the state, two of them private. Table 2.9 lists the courses that transfer from Lee College to various four-year institutions. These statistics are for courses offered, not sections, and are not directly comparable to other statistics in this study. The percentages do illustrate, however, differences among institutions that accept courses from one community college.

Several findings from Table 2.9 are worth comment. First, the two private universities have much lower transferability rates than all but one of the public institutions. Second, the wide disparity between transferability rates to the four-year institutions (from a high of 97.4 percent for all courses offered to a low of 14.2 percent) may be accounted for by two factors influencing articulation agreements: the proximity between the two- and four-year institutions and the ability of the community college articulation officer to build a relationship with a university's transfer coordinator. Lee College in Baytown, Texas, is a considerable distance from the four-year institution where it has its lowest transferability percentage of 14.2 percent, Texas Tech in Lubbock. And third, the differences between transferability of all courses offered and just the non–liberal arts courses range from a high of 20.7 percentage points to a low of 0.4 percent. In one instance, the non–liberal arts actually transfer at a slightly higher percentage than all courses offered, 93.5 percent to 93.3 percent at the University of Houston–Main. Overall, there do not appear to be

Table 2.9. Courses that Transfer from Lee College

	All Courses Offered	Non–Liberal Arts Courses
Public Four-Year Institutions		
Sam Houston State University	45.7%	27.5%
Texas A & M University	36.9	16.2
University of Houston–Clear Lake	28.8	15.8
University of Houston–Downtown	52.8	33.8
University of Houston–Main	93.3	93.5
Stephen F. Austin State University	46.9	28.9
University of Texas–Austin	40.6	21.6
Texas Tech	14.2	5.5
Southwest Texas State University	97.4	97.3
Lamar	41.6	21.2
University of North Texas	73.2	64.4
East Texas State Universtiy	92.9	92.2
Texas Woman's University	62.9	50.8
Private Four-Year Institutions		
Baylor	12.7	2.5
Houston Baptist	11.6	6.5

wide differences between transferability rates of all courses offered and just the non–liberal arts.

What Transfers in Illinois? Three Illinois community colleges provided data on non–liberal arts transferability to Illinois State University and to the state's flagship research institution, the University of Illinois at Urbana-Champaign. Transfer guides were obtained from the Illinois Community College Board and used to calculate transferability percentages.

The degree to which the various non–liberal arts subject areas transfer follows a pattern similar to that of California's, although the pattern is even more pronounced in Illinois (Table 2.10). The University of Illinois research university showed higher selectivity than the University of California system in accepting non–liberal arts courses for credit (15.9 percent to 28.9 percent, respectively) and Illinois State University displayed a considerably higher rate of acceptance of non–liberal arts courses for transfer than did the California State University system (80.4 percent to 61.7 percent, respectively). Two subject areas that yielded different results in Illinois, however, were the high percentage of trade and industry courses that transferred to Illinois State University (86.9 percent) compared to that which transferred to the California State University system (35.7 percent), and the comparatively low transferability rate of personal skills courses, largely physical education courses, to the University of Illinois (49.5 percent) compared to the University of California system results (76.7 percent). For several subject areas, data were too sparse to report. In general, data for Illinois should be considered preliminary, since only three community colleges furnished complete data for analysis.

Table 2.10. Non–Liberal Arts Transferability Rates in Illinois Community Colleges

Transfer Subject Area	Illinois State University	University of Illinois–Urbana-Champaign
Agriculture	100.0%	0%
Business and office	78.7	30.9
Marketing and distribution	91.5	0
Health	29.8	.9
Home economics	N.A.	N.A.
Technical education	97.2	7.3
Engineering technology	100.0	0
Trade and industry	86.9	4.8
Personal skills and avocational courses	89.2	49.5
Education	92.9	17.9
Other	N.A.	N.A.
Overall Transferability	80.4%	15.9

Note: N = 3.

What General Patterns Are Discernible from the Transferability Data? Similarities exist in the overall transferability patterns for Illinois and California, although substantial differences also emerge between the two states in transferability percentages for specific disciplines. The following very general observations are possible: Research universities are considerably more selective in accepting non–liberal arts courses for transfer credit; personal skills and avocational courses tend to transfer at a high rate, largely because of physical education courses; trade and industry courses do not transfer at a high rate, except to Illinois State University; and health occupations courses also tend to have comparatively low transferability rates.

The overall pattern for Texas, however, is considerably different than for the other two states. Texas four-year institutions seem to accept non–liberal arts courses for transfer at much more similar rates to the state universities and to the flagship research institution (41.6 percent and 35.3 percent).

Summary

This chapter has reported the findings of the most recent of a series of studies of the liberal arts curriculum in American community colleges. Findings were that, overall, the liberal arts have expanded from 52 percent of the total curriculum in 1986 to 56 percent in 1991. This probably resulted less from the introduction of new courses or course requirements than from an increase in the proportion of students seeking the first two years of baccalaureate study and in state requirements for the liberal arts in all degree programs. The enrollment figures show the continued dominance of the traditional general education courses: English composition, introductory math, psychology, history, and political science. The most notable shift in the curriculum was in foreign languages, where, fueled by a notable jump in ESL enrollments and in the number of colleges offering ESL, the foreign languages share rose from 5 to 8.5 percent of the entire set of liberal arts classes.

Relationships between the liberal arts curriculum and college size and location were analyzed. Colleges in urban areas were found to offer higher percentages of remedial courses, thus confirming a generally accepted notion. College size was related to course patterns only in the provision of specialized classes: the larger the college, the more likely that a class in, for example, dance or cultural geography would be found. (A similar relationship appeared in the earlier studies.) A community college must have quite a large student body before it has the enrollment sufficient to support specialized classes in many fields.

For the non–liberal arts, general findings indicate that courses in trade and industry do not transfer at high percentages but personal skills and avocational courses do, largely because of physical education courses. The second major finding is that research universities are more selective in the non–liberal arts courses they accept for transfer credit. This is especially true in California and Illinois, but less so in Texas. The third finding concerns the overall transferability of the non–liberal arts. Except for trade and industry courses, the concept of "terminal education" should be laid to rest.

Notes

1. Throughout this chapter, *transferability* refers to course transferability from community colleges to four-year institutions; *transfer* refers to student transfers.
2. Research Universities I and Comprehensive Universities and Colleges I were defined in this study using the definitions in the 1987 edition of the Carnegie Foundation's *A Classification of Institutions of Higher Education,* p. 7.

References

Carnegie Foundation for the Advancement of Teaching. *A Classification of Institutions of Higher Education.* Princeton, N.J.: Carnegie Foundation for the Advancement of Teaching, 1987.

Cohen, A. M., and Brawer, F. B. *The Collegiate Function of Community Colleges.* San Francisco: Jossey-Bass, 1987.

Cohen, A. M., and Brawer, F. B. *The American Community College.* (2nd ed.) San Francisco: Jossey-Bass, 1989.

Grubb, N. *The Postsecondary Education of 1972 Seniors Completing Vocational A.A. Degrees and Certificates.* Berkeley, Calif.: MPR Associates, 1987.

Grubb, N. "The Decline of Community College Transfer Rates: Evidence from National Longitudinal Surveys." *Journal of Higher Education,* 1991, *62* (2), 194–222.

Levine, A., and Cureton, J. "The Quiet Revolution: Eleven Facts About Multiculturalism and the Curriculum." *Change,* 1992, *24* (1), 25–29.

Richardson, R., and Bender, L. *Students in Urban Settings: Achieving the Baccalaureate Degree.* Washington, D.C.: Association for the Study of Higher Education, 1985.

ARTHUR M. COHEN is director of the ERIC Clearinghouse for Community Colleges and professor of higher education at the University of California, Los Angeles.

JAN M. IGNASH is a research assistant at the Center for the Study of Community Colleges and a doctoral candidate in higher education at the University of California, Los Angeles.

Which liberal arts subjects in the community college curriculum have remained relatively stable over the past sixteen years and which have increased or decreased?

Stability and Change in the Liberal Arts Curriculum

Barry VanderKelen

The community colleges serve five functions: to provide the first two years of postsecondary education in preparation for student transfer to baccalaureate degree-granting institutions; to provide general education to people who would not have access to such courses otherwise; to prepare people to enter the work force with specific job-related skills; to increase students' abilities to cope with college-level courses (Clowes, 1984, p. 156); and to upgrade the skills and credentials of people already in the work force. Courses and programs of study are central to all these functions. The study of community colleges' curricula is important, therefore, to the assessment of how the colleges are serving their constituencies.

Tying the functions together is the liberal arts curriculum. The liberal arts encompass such a wide range of subjects that most students take liberal arts courses at some time in their plan of study. The liberal arts represent the historical roots of the community colleges; they are the main factor differentiating community colleges from proprietary schools. The liberal arts are at the heart of the community college mission to serve as a link between elementary and secondary schools and establishments of higher learning. The strength of the link rests on the transfer function and the general education function. The liberal arts serve as the core of transferable credits and provide students with the first two years of a baccalaureate program. Also, the liberal arts provide a distribution of classes to those who seek vocational training or retraining, or who enroll because they are interested in the subject.

The discussion in this chapter provides an overview of the state of the liberal arts curriculum in the American community college with attention to stability and change over the period of 1975–1991.

NEW DIRECTIONS FOR COMMUNITY COLLEGES, no. 86, Summer 1994 © Jossey-Bass Publishers

Liberal Arts Versus General Education

It is important to distinguish between the concepts of liberal arts and general education. The differences have grown subtle over time and the roots of the concepts have blurred, leading to the terms being used interchangeably. However, as studies conducted by the Center for the Study of Community Colleges (CSCC) have shown, enrollment patterns in courses point to practical as well as philosophical differences.

Idealistic definitions of the liberal arts address such things as passing on the culture to succeeding generations and exposing students to the unique world views and problem-solving methods of the various disciplines that make up the liberal arts. The humanities are emphasized in the liberal arts since the humanities capture the culture of the civilization that is to be passed along; in the United States the dominant culture of the humanities is the thought and tradition of Western civilization. The liberal arts help us in our search for truth and help us understand what it means to be human (Herzberg, 1984). Put another way, the liberal arts free the mind for growth and maturity, helping students to lead satisfying lives. American higher education inherited the liberal arts from its English ancestors. The classical curriculum of the colonial colleges included the study of Latin, to prepare students for the ministry, and Greek, to prepare students to be scholars and gentlemen (Rudolph, 1962, p. 23). But as the character of knowledge changed and the needs of society changed, vocational aims beyond the ministry were introduced into the curriculum. The classical curriculum became impractical and awkward. In response to creeping vocationalism, general education requirements were introduced to keep programs of study rooted in the aristocratic ideal of the classical curriculum (Rudolph, 1962, p. 455).

General education, then, might be thought of as a pragmatic incarnation of the classical curriculum. Central to the notion of general education is the enculturation of students. Rather than have students study nothing but culture vis-à-vis the classical curriculum, general education ensures that each student has enough breadth of courses to cultivate understanding of the different ways of thought of the academic disciplines. Clowes (1984, p. 156) states three aspects of general education: building skills for advanced studies and life-long learning; exposing students to the mainstream thought and interpretation of the humanities, sciences, social sciences, and the arts; and cultivating students' broad understanding and ability to think about a large and complex subject.

The landmark report *General Education in a Free Society* (1952) stated that it is imperative that all students be required to study the liberal arts. By doing so, a common base is established from which every person can consider and address the responsibilities and challenges of living in a democracy (pp. 52–53).

What of the Curriculum to Study?

Choosing what aspects of the curriculum to study is a matter of great debate because curriculum can be thought of as a plan of courses which leads students to a degree, or the sequence of courses which students take; what is offered and what students take may not be the same. Beauchamp (1981, p. 7) suggests even a third conceptualization of the term curriculum, that curriculum is a system within which decisions are made about what the curriculum will be and how it will be implemented. The curriculum system includes the negotiations that are inherent in any college's academic decision-making process. Analyzing a college's curriculum is not as simple as reviewing the stated requirements for a degree.

The printed curriculum that colleges offer in their official bulletins and manuals represents more of a philosophical statement of purpose than the "real" curriculum. Studying the printed curriculum would present an analysis of what the colleges *profess* to be. On the other hand, Zemsky (1989) and Clowes (1984), among others, argue that the "real" curriculum is what students actually take and what is actually taught. But attempts to measure what is taught often fail because of the problem of defining breadth and depth of each course and each sequence of courses. How can the researcher be sure that a history course on the Civil War in one college is the same as another? This study is not a content analysis of the courses; rather, it is an analysis of the courses actually offered and the enrollments in those courses.

English

English courses offered by community colleges include composition courses, reading classes, speech classes, and business communication courses. English courses serve the transfer, general education, worker preparation, and remediation functions of the community college curriculum. Almost all of the colleges surveyed, 99 percent, offered English courses, and approximately 21 percent of all liberal arts courses offered are English classes. More than one in every five enrollments in liberal arts courses is in an English course.

Writing classes are the most frequently offered English courses. Of the colleges surveyed, 84 percent offered remedial composition classes, almost all, 97 percent, offered standard-level composition courses, and three-quarters offered advanced composition courses. Almost three-quarters of the colleges offered remedial reading classes, while eight percent offered advanced reading classes. One out of five of the colleges offered advanced business communication courses.

Approximately a third of the English courses offered in 1991 were at the remedial level. Interestingly, this proportion remains unchanged from the 1986 study. These data suggest that community colleges are actively addressing adult literacy needs, as well as serving transfer and vocational functions.

Fine and Performing Arts

The fine and performing arts include dance, music, theater, and visual arts. The arts both serve performance-based education needs and help students to envision multiple solutions to problems and seek the meaning of situations.

Almost one-quarter of the fine and performing arts courses were painting and drawing courses (visual arts), another 20 percent were handicrafts (visual arts), and 17 percent were instrument training (music).

Not surprisingly, none of the colleges included in the study offered reme-dial fine and performing arts courses; as with social science courses, it would be difficult to define a remedial level mastery of the arts. All of the colleges offered advanced classes in each of the subject areas, and two-thirds of the col-leges offered advanced classes in the visual arts. Fine and performing arts courses accounted for only about five percent of the liberal arts enrollments, with over half, 52 percent, of the enrollments being in visual arts courses. Interestingly, this percentage dropped from 1986 to 1991. In 1986, fine and performing arts courses accounted for 13 percent of all liberal arts courses, while in 1991 they accounted for 9.6 percent. The largest drop in colleges offering courses was in music, with fewer community colleges offering courses in instruments (down 7 percent), theory (down 2 percent), and voice (down 2 percent). Overall, though, music courses capture nearly one-third of all enrollments in fine and performing arts courses.

More community colleges offered courses in painting/drawing in 1991 than in 1986 (up 10 percent), and in handicrafts (up 4 percent). The same pro-portion of colleges offered dance (6 percent) and theater (4 percent) in 1991 as did in 1986. The increases in visual arts and the stability of dance and the-ater suggest more general interest enrollments than enrollments due to voca-tional or transfer students, and counter claims of decreasing interest in performance-based arts.

Humanities

The humanities help us to better understand what it means to be human, and are the primary means of preserving and transmitting culture to future gener-ations. The humanities include art history, cultural anthropology, cultural geog-raphy, foreign languages, history, literature, fine and performing arts history and appreciation, philosophy, political science, religious studies, and social and ethnic studies.

Humanities courses accounted for approximately 27 percent of all liberal arts enrollments, with 27 percent of the humanities enrollments in foreign language courses. Only a couple of the colleges included in the survey offered remedial courses in interdisciplinary humanities, usually high school level classes in government or civics. A noticeable percentage of colleges offered advanced literature classes, 29 percent, and advanced political science classes, 21 percent.

Table 3.1 shows that the humanities have been remarkably consistent over the course of sixteen years. A few observations are warranted.

First, although the frequency of colleges offering foreign languages has remained high, the proportion of liberal arts classes that are foreign languages has almost doubled. In 1991, foreign language classes accounted for 36 percent of the total humanities class sections, an increase from 21 percent in 1977. This increase is due primarily to the number of English as a Second Language courses offered and points to the community colleges' role as points of entry for immigrants. Chapter Five deals with this in depth.

Second, philosophy has been able to increase its visibility by the addition of logic classes primarily for computer science students and ethics classes for all students. The increase in philosophy due to logic classes is linked to the increase in computer science as seen in the mathematics section.

Third, the increase in the number of colleges offering interdisciplinary humanities courses, combined with the decrease in social and ethnic studies, suggests that community colleges are introducing multiculturalism into the curriculum through existing programs and departments rather than through the creation of new programs and departments.

Table 3.1   Humanities Instruction in Two-Year Colleges

	Percentage of Colleges Offering Courses				
Broad Subject Area	1975 (n = 156)	1977 (n = 178)	1983 (n = 173)	1986 (n = 95)	1991 (n = 164)
Cultural anthropology	44%	46%	44%	48%	47%
Art history/appreciation	70	68	76	76	80
Foreign languages	82	80	82	78	87
Cultural geography	26	22	34	NA	24
History	90	92	93	92	92
Literature	91	92	93	87	92
Interdisciplinary	28	28	38	52	48
Music appreciation	74	70	69	63	71
Philosophy	66	64	68	76	79
Political science	89	94	90	86	90
Religious studies	26	28	24	[a]	22
Social and ethnic studies	22	21	10	[b]	15

[a] Included in Philosophy.

[b] Included in History and Literature.

Mathematics

Mathematics has been a part of the curriculum from the very beginning of American higher education. Access was limited in the early days, and students were not allowed to study mathematics until their fourth year of study (Rudolph, 1962, p. 25). But mathematics was the first subject to break Latin and Greek's reign as the measure of a student's readiness to study the collegiate curriculum (Rudolph, 1962, p. 29).

The 1991 CSCC curriculum study found that almost every community college (98 percent) offered mathematics courses, and that nearly one out of every five liberal arts courses offered was a mathematics course.

Mathematics serves every function of the curriculum. Some 63 percent of the colleges surveyed offered remedial courses in introductory and intermediate mathematics; this suggests that community colleges are actively addressing numeracy needs. These courses are typically pre-algebra or introductory algebra courses. A slightly higher percentage of the colleges, 67 percent, offered advanced courses in computer science, typically programming classes, that are largely vocationally oriented. Another 60 percent of the colleges offered advanced courses in calculus, while just over half the colleges, 51 percent, offered advanced courses in introductory and intermediate mathematics, in an attempt to prepare students for transfer. Just under 20 percent of the liberal arts enrollment is found in mathematics courses. Table 3.2 details the percentages of colleges offering mathematics courses offered over the years.

The large drop in colleges offering applied mathematics/technology-related courses might be linked to the drop in the engineering courses in the science

Table 3.2   Mathematics Instruction in Two-Year Colleges

Broad Subject Area	Percentage of Colleges Offering Courses			Percentage of Enrollment	
	1978 (n = 175)	1986 (n = 95)	1991 (n = 164)	All Liberal Arts Courses, 1991	All Mathematics Courses, 1991
Introductory and intermediate mathematics	97%	97%	98%	12.0%	63.2%
Advanced mathematics	86	87	86	1.4	7.2
Applied technology-related mathematics	67	64	57	0.7	3.4
Computer science	71	88	90	2.3	12.2
Math for other majors	95	77	81	1.6	8.2
Statistics	75	78	79	1.1	5.7

departments. The fluctuation in the colleges offering math for other majors suggests that the placement of required mathematics courses might shift with changing needs of academic programs.

Science

The sciences include agriculture and natural resources, biology, engineering, chemistry, earth and space science, and physics. Science classes serve the transfer, general education, and worker preparation functions of the community college curriculum (Clowes, 1984, p. 156). Very few colleges offer remedial science classes: 4.3 percent offer remedial chemistry courses and 1.2 percent offer remedial integrated science courses.

Sciences elbowed their way into the curriculum as the scientific method became more accepted. The introduction of the sciences at about the time of the American Revolution (Rudolph, 1962, p. 30) was a contributing factor to the demise of the classical curriculum. The most direct link between the sciences today and the classical curriculum is physics. Biology, chemistry, and the other sciences developed out of advances in knowledge fostered by the scientific method.

Science courses accounted for approximately fourteen percent of all liberal arts enrollments in 1991, and almost one-half of the science enrollments are in biology courses.

Table 3.3 shows that almost half of the science enrollments are in biology courses. Almost all of the colleges offered standard-level biology courses in 1991, while over 68 percent offered advanced biology courses, the largest offering of advanced science courses. Meeting science credit requirements for transfer helps account for such a large biology enrollment, but because only one in five community college students transfers to baccalaureate institutions, allied health vocational training and retraining must make up a large portion of the biology enrollment.

Colleges offered remedial science courses only in chemistry and integrated science; 4.3 percent of the colleges offered remedial chemistry in 1991 and 1.2 percent offered remedial integrated science courses. Standard-level chemistry courses were offered by 82.9 percent of the colleges, the second largest offering in the standard category. However, the enrollment in chemistry courses was not nearly that of the enrollment in biology courses. This might suggest that non-science majors opt to take biology lectures or labs instead of chemistry lectures or labs, and that chemistry courses are more geared toward vocational programs than the broader based biology offerings.

The decrease in the number of colleges offering engineering courses may be a reflection of a national decrease in engineering enrollments, or of a shift of engineering courses to upper-division programs at four-year institutions.

Table 3.3. Science Instruction in Two-Year Colleges

Broad Subject Area	Percentage of Colleges Offering Courses			Percentage of Enrollment	
	1978 (n = 175)	1986 (n = 95)	1991 (n = 164)	All Liberal Arts Courses, 1991	All Science Courses, 1991
Agriculture and natural science	61%	52%	16%[a]	N.A.	N.A.
Biology	100	98	95	6.4%	46.6%
Chemistry	97	96	93	2.0	15.0
Engineering	81	72	50	1.6	11.7
Earth and space science	79	72	72	1.3	9.8
Physics	89	92	87	1.3	9.2
Other				1.1	7.8

[a] The sharp drop in the number of colleges offering courses in agriculture and natural resources may be due to sampling error.

The decrease in the number of colleges offering applied/technology-related mathematics courses and to a lesser extent physics courses means engineers are not enrolling in those courses either. The decrease in the number of students studying engineering has generated concern for future engineering labor force needs. Krogh (1989) estimates that as many as three out of four engineers who are needed to fill the projected engineering jobs in the year 2000 are already in the workforce (p. 36). In 1986, the National Science Board found that 92 percent of eligible engineers were employed in the workforce (NSB, 1989, p. 71). The decreasing pool of available engineers and the high participation rate in the field by trained engineers suggests an opportunity for community colleges to serve the engineering community by offering retraining and continuing education in technology-related fields. Such a sharp drop in community colleges offering engineering courses merits further investigation.

Social Sciences

The social sciences include psychology, sociology, economics, geography, and anthropology. Tracing their roots back to the moral philosophy component of the classical curriculum, the social sciences accounted for approximately fifteen percent of all liberal arts course enrollments in the community colleges in 1991.

Almost all colleges surveyed offered social science courses, especially courses in economics, psychology, and sociology. Less than half the colleges offered courses in geography, interdisciplinary social science, and anthropol-

Table 3.4. Social Science Instruction in Two-Year Colleges

Broad Subject Area	Percentage of Colleges Offering Courses			Percentage of Enrollment	
	1978 (n = 175)	1986 (n = 95)	1991 (n = 164)	All Liberal Arts Courses, 1991	All Science Courses, 1991
Anthropology and interdisciplinary social science	67%	53%	64%	1.2%	8.1%
Psychology	99	100	98	7.2	47.3
Economics	99	97	93	2.7	18.0
Sociology	100	95	94	4.0	26.2

ogy. None of the courses offered were classified as remedial. Almost one-half of the social science enrollments were in psychology courses. Table 3.4 details the frequency of social science course offerings over a period of thirteen years.

The large proportion of social science enrollments in psychology courses requires further review. In 1991, less than half the colleges offered courses in the sub-subject areas of abnormal, social/industrial, personality/adjustment, experimental, educational, contemporary issues, and physiological psychology, while almost all colleges offered courses in elementary/general and developmental psychology. This suggests a return to the basics.

Since 1978, fewer community colleges are offering psychology courses in social/industrial, personality/adjustment, experimental, educational, and contemporary issues; more community colleges are offering courses in developmental and physiological psychology; and about the same number of colleges are offering courses in elementary/general and abnormal psychology. Furthermore, psychology instructors have reported that it is more important to develop a student's self-understanding than to develop a knowledge or skill-base that would be useful in the further study of psychology.

Specialized courses and advanced courses are often not accepted by baccalaureate institutions as transferable credits, forcing students to take elementary and general-level courses. The decline in specialized courses and instructor reports of promoting self-understanding suggest that the content of the elementary/general courses has changed to address issues previously covered in more specialized courses, including personality/adjustment. In other words, the psychology courses may have become more utilitarian for the students while they have maintained the guise of transferable credits.

Not surprisingly, no community colleges offered remedial social science courses; it would be difficult to define a compensatory, developmental, or below-college proficiency in the social sciences. Social science departments, however, could help remediate skills by offering developmental courses based on its subject areas by focusing on reading, writing, or critical thinking development. At the other end of the spectrum, less than one in seven community colleges offered advanced courses in the social sciences.

These patterns suggest that the primary motivation for students to enroll in psychology courses is for personal interest.

Table 3.5 shows that six subject areas, English, foreign language, psychology, biology, history, and introductory and intermediate mathematics make up almost 60 percent of liberal arts enrollments. These six subjects, then, represent the core of the current liberal arts curriculum in community colleges.

Conclusion

This chapter began by stating that the study of the community college curriculum is important for the assessment of whether or not the colleges are serving their constituencies. The liberal arts, which tie together all of the functions of the courses and programs of study, account for over half of all courses offered by community colleges. A review of the liberal arts, then, assists us in the assessment of community colleges and their ability to meet the needs of their constituents.

Data on the liberal arts, as collected by the CSCC over 16 years, show that the liberal arts' strength, as measured by the number of courses offered, the breadth of courses offered, and the enrollment in those courses, as well as their flexibility allow community colleges to meet the changing needs of their constituencies. Vocationalism has been absorbed somewhat by expanding mathematics to include computer science, thereby helping some students prepare for transfer to baccalaureate institutions while preparing others for entry into the workforce. Other examples of flexibility include offering remedial English and mathematics courses to help address adult literacy and numeracy needs,

Table 3.5. Top Enrollments in Subject Areas as a Percentage
of Total Liberal Arts Enrollments, 1991

English	20.0%
Introductory and intermediate mathematics	12.0
Foreign language	7.2
Psychology	7.2
Biology	6.4
History	5.8
Total	58.6%

and offering English as a Second Language in foreign language departments to help immigrants become established in the United States.

Probably the most striking evidence of the central role of the liberal arts in the overall curriculum is the large number of enrollments the liberal arts capture. On a duplicated head-count basis, more than 6.3 million students enrolled in liberal arts classes during spring 1991.

The liberal arts in the community colleges, as measured by the courses actually offered and enrollment in those courses, are central to the colleges' ability to meet the needs of their constituents, and remain the focus of the overall curriculum.

References

Beauchamp, G. A. *Curriculum Theory.* (4th ed.) Itasca, Ill.: Peacock, 1981.

Clowes, D. A. "Functions of the Two-Year College Curriculum: Faculty Perceptions." *Community/Junior College Quarterly of Research and Practice,* 1984, *8,* 155–167.

General Education in a Free Society: Report of the Harvard Committee. Cambridge, Mass.: Harvard University Press, 1952.

Herzberg, G. "Science and Culture." Address presented at Honors Day Convocation, University of Toledo, Toledo, Ohio, May 1984.

Krogh, L. C. "How One Company Is Facing the Challenges of the Future." *Engineering Education,* 1989, *79* (Jan./Feb.), 36–38.

National Science Board. *Science and Engineering Indicators, 1989.* NSB 89–1. Washington, D.C.: U.S. Government Printing Office, 1989.

Rudolph, F. *The American College and University: A History.* New York: Random House, 1962.

Zemsky, R. *Structure and Coherence: Measuring the Undergraduate Curriculum.* Washington, D.C.: Association of American Colleges, 1989.

BARRY VANDERKELEN is director of development at Loyola Law School and a doctoral student in higher education at the University of California, Los Angeles.

Do associate degree completion requirements or stated requirements relate to the curriculum? Is there a pattern between what colleges offer and graduation requirements?

Graduation Requirements, General Education, and the Liberal Arts

Charles R. Brinkman IV

Is there a pattern between what community colleges offer and what they require for graduation? It would seem so, but because less than one in five matriculants obtains an associate degree, the curriculum may well be divergent. Although not all students attend community colleges to complete the associate degree, does the curriculum present a realistic opportunity to obtain this degree? What types of courses are required for associate degrees and how do students meet these requirements? The collection of related data by the Center for the Study of Community Colleges presents an opportunity to examine this issue. When examining graduation requirements, it is beneficial to understand how the community college curriculum and graduation requirements developed.

The community college liberal arts curriculum was inherited from the four-year college. Only in a very few interdisciplinary liberal arts studies that fall within the humanities are the community colleges innovative. The community colleges, in their early-century attempt to link themselves with the universities and drop the label of high school extension, accepted the curriculum of the universities as the quickest way to become university-like. More than half of all credit courses in the community colleges are liberal arts, due to the university influence. The universities hold the community colleges accountable for their courses by constantly reviewing courses to ensure equivalency with university lower-division courses. Thus the associate-degree graduation requirements of the community colleges reflect the university influence. The same courses serve as general education requirements for students who transfer in order to obtain their baccalaureate.

It is in the interest of all faculty, both university and community college, to have their courses required for graduation in the distribution, or general education, requirements. Required courses lead to academic power for the faculty teaching that subject. This common interest often led these institutions to come together statewide and mandate graduation requirements in many instances. In state after state, 20–40 units of liberal arts are required for graduation, in both the community college and university.

The topic of graduation requirements has been reviewed. A report by Laurie L. Lewis titled "Requirements in Undergraduate General Education" (1992) looked at obligatory general education requirements for undergraduates at two-year and four-year colleges. This report found that 90 percent of the two-year colleges required some general education courses in order to receive a degree. Other studies report that 96 percent of two-year institutions have some sort of general education requirements (Ottinger, 1987), but they may be different for students with differing goals. Neal Raisman (1992) examined general education within the Michigan community college system. Although the 29 two-year colleges are all independent of any centralized control and can thus structure their own general education requirements within the college, he found much similarity across the state.

Community colleges enroll 45.5 percent of all undergraduate students in higher education. This percentage varies greatly by state. Some states, such as California, where the community colleges enroll 71 percent of all beginning students, are much higher than average, and others, especially those in the Northeast, are quite a bit lower (*Chronicle of Higher Education Almanac*, 1993, pp. 5, 52). Although 5,181,000 students were enrolled in community colleges throughout the United States in Fall 1990, approximately 481,700 associate degrees were awarded during 1990–1991 (*Chronicle of Higher Education Almanac*, 1992, p. 3; 1993, p. 5). Therefore graduation requirements should not drive the curriculum. But do they?

Liberal Arts, General Education, and Graduation Requirements

Several influences lead to a commonality of general education requirements, both statewide and "interstate."

Academic respectability. Colleges do not want to be seen as too different or deviant from the mainstream; therefore they try to make their requirements similar to the higher education system as a whole. Even college systems that are not centralized in their general education requirements are often quite similar. This makes it easier for students who do transfer within community colleges to meet the general education requirements of the community college where they eventually get a degree. Community colleges that are not close to the norm in their general education requirements are seen as different, and often have difficulty in some areas of academic respectability, such as accreditation, discussed below.

Horizontal and vertical transfer. The horizontal transfer, moving between community colleges, is facilitated if general education requirements are similar. Since most community college students are transitory, dropping in and out of school over periods of time, if different colleges have similar general education requirements, this horizontal movement of the students is facilitated. The occasional student may thus obtain a degree over a period of time, at different locations.

Vertical transfer, from community colleges to four-year institutions, is an accounting method. The four-year institutions continually monitor the courses completed at the community colleges to ensure that they are comparable to their own courses, and thus hold the community colleges accountable for meshing the curriculum. This also lends itself to the commonality of general education requirements as seen across the community college spectrum. The community and local four-year colleges should both have similar general education requirements, as a further meshing of the curriculum. This is beneficial to the community college students who plan to transfer to a four-year college. This way, they can meet the requirements for an associate degree and bachelor's degree at the same time.

Accrediting bodies. The various regional accrediting organizations also encourage homogeneity of general education requirements across the community college spectrum. These accrediting organizations look for certain standards that the colleges must meet in order to keep their accreditation. Colleges that are quite different from the established norms have more to explain to the accreditation team. Thus, the accrediting process, which occurs every few years, also lends itself to creating a similarity of general education patterns between colleges, facilitating student movement.

How might accrediting teams judge whether the curriculum and the graduation requirements are similar? Several approaches are possible. First, individual colleges can be examined to see if they offer enough class sections in the appropriate general education requirements for their students to complete the associate degree. Next, the graduation and degree requirements of community colleges within each state can be examined because these requirements are often mandated statewide. There should be enough course offerings throughout the state to fill the need for these requirements. Finally, the graduation requirements of community colleges as a whole can be explored to ensure that needed courses are offered in acceptable proportions to facilitate graduation. If we find that almost all community colleges require a U.S. history or U.S. government course for graduation, we should also find that practically all colleges offer such courses.

Findings

The sample of 164 community colleges in the Center for the Study of Community Colleges' (CSCC) 1991 study was further narrowed down to look at the graduation requirements of 40 community colleges as a representative subsample, taking the size of the college into account and using states as a sampling variable. This chapter explores the graduation requirements of community colleges within several states, looking at the curriculum and graduation requirements overall, to see how the curriculum offered relates to the necessary graduation requirements. Using the data from the CSCC curriculum study, it investigates whether community colleges really offer the courses students need to receive an associate degree.

Looking at the graduation requirements listed in the community college catalogs reveals much similarity. Almost all colleges require an English composition course, some kind of math proficiency, 3 or more units in social science courses (which is often U.S. history or U.S. government), humanities or fine arts courses, and, finally, some kind of natural science course or courses. Also, most colleges require a health or a physical education course for the associate degree. A few colleges require an ethnic studies course for graduation, and others require a computer literacy course. Although the number of colleges that require ethnic studies and computer literacy courses will probably rise in the future, in 1991 that number was quite small. Table 4.1 summarizes these data.

The percentages shown in Table 4.1 closely match what other studies have found. Based on the guidelines for students entering community colleges in 1988–1989, Laurie Lewis (1992) found that 94 percent of the schools required English composition, 68 percent required social sciences, and 64 percent required math. All these percentages were up from a 1983–1984 study.

The general education requirements can vary, depending on the type of associate degree. The degrees offered by some of the colleges examined included, among others, the Associate of Arts, Associate of Science, Associate of Applied Science, Associate of General Science, and Associate of Liberal Science.

Table 4.2 shows the total enrollment figures for the liberal arts courses. It reveals that most students use certain courses to satisfy the general education requirements within broad subject areas, including humanities, science, social science, and mathematics. Students seem to use foreign languages, history, and polit-

Table 4.1. Percentage of Community Colleges That Require Various Subjects for General Education Graduation Requirements

Subject	Percentage
English composition	97%
Math	97
Humanities	88
Social studies	98
U.S. history	34
U.S. government	26
Natural science	94
Physical education/health	74
Ethnic studies	8
Computer literacy	11

Note: $n = 40$.

Table 4.2. Total Spring 1991 Student Enrollment Figures for All Liberal Arts Areas

Humanities	
Art history/appreciation	84,700
Cultural anthropology	31,100
Foreign languages	460,700
History	396,500
Interdisciplinary humanities (includes cultural geography)	94,200
Literature	120,900
Fine and performing arts history/appreciation	29,900
Music history/appreciation	65,600
Philosophy and logic	143,200
Political science	249,000
Religious studies	14,300
Social/ethnic studies	13,400
English	1,317,400
Fine and Performing Arts	
Dance	27,600
Music	95,800
Theater	19,600
Visual arts	151,700
Social Sciences	
Anthropology	28,000
Economics	173,500
Geography	19,500
Interdisciplinary social sciences	30,100
Psychology	455,100
Sociology	256,300
Sciences	
Agricultural science/natural resources	[a]
Biological sciences	405,500
Chemistry	130,200
Earth and space sciences (includes environmental science)	85,100
Engineering sciences and technology	102,200
Geology	24,100
Integrated science	43,400
Physics	80,100
Mathematics and Computer Sciences	
Introductory and intermediate mathematics	766,100
Advanced mathematics	87,700
Applied math/technology-related	41,600
Computer science technology	147,200
Math for other majors	99,700
Statistics and probability	69,000

[a] Too small to report.

ical science most often to satisfy the humanities requirement, while introductory and intermediate math courses are used to satisfy the mathematics requirement. Psychology, sociology, and economics are used to meet the social science requirement, while biology is the most popular course to meet the science requirement.

Conclusions

It appears that the general education requirements for community college graduation match quite well what the colleges are offering as part of their curriculum. The general education requirements are often standardized within the state, so we expected to see that an appropriate percentage of the necessary classes required for graduation were offered. This appears to be the case. When colleges require a course, the student has many options to choose from to meet this requirement. Even though the general education requirements may be standardized, the community colleges in the same state still have some flexibility as far as graduation requirements are concerned. In those states with a large number of community colleges, the general education, and other requirements, are often very similar.

This match between the general education requirements of community colleges and their curricular offerings facilitates transfer between colleges and enhances the ease with which a student may obtain an associate degree. If the general education pattern at community colleges matches that at four-year institutions, students who complete the general education requirements at the community colleges can use those credits to transfer to four-year schools. Therefore, the availability of general education courses at the community colleges serves more purposes than to facilitate graduation from the two-year institution. Community college students may not realize this, but the meshing of the two- and four-year college general education curriculum is to their distinct advantage. Due to the historical significance of this meshing and the continuation of the process, many community college students have been able to get their start in higher education and continue to progress up the ladder toward higher degrees.

References

Chronicle of Higher Education Almanac, Washington, D.C.: Chronicle of Higher Education, 1992.
Chronicle of Higher Education Almanac, Washington, D.C.: Chronicle of Higher Education, 1993.
Lewis, L. L. *Requirements in Undergraduate General Education.* Washingtion, D.C.: Westat, 1992.
Ottinger, C. A. (ed.). *Higher Education Today: Facts in Brief.* Washington, D.C.: American Council on Education, 1987.
Raisman, N. A. *"The Defacto State of General Education in Michigan Community Colleges".* In N. A. Raisman (ed.), *Directing General Education Outcomes.* New Directions for Community Colleges, no. 81. San Francisco: Jossey-Bass, 1993.

CHARLES R. BRINKMAN IV is a counselor at Santa Monica College in California. He is working on a doctoral degree in higher education at the University of California, Los Angeles.

Why has there been a tremendous surge in the need for English as a Second Language courses, and what policy implications does this have for community colleges?

Compelling Numbers: English as a Second Language

Jan M. Ignash

At Passaic County Community College in New Jersey, 35 percent of the student population took at least one English as a Second Language (ESL) class during spring session 1991. At El Paso Community College a conservative estimate calculated that 11 percent of the student population took an ESL course *for credit*, with 429 credit and 179 noncredit sections offered to meet the demand for ESL. In 1991, 800 Russian immigrants showed up en masse at Harry S. Truman College in Chicago requesting ESL classes. While these three community colleges are among the nation's largest in terms of ESL enrollments and number of ESL sections offered, they indicate the tremendous growth of ESL in many urban community colleges and in a small but growing number of more rural colleges as well.

The first section of this chapter describes the results of the Spring 1991 National Curriculum Study conducted by the Center for the Study of Community Colleges (CSCC) as related to ESL and compares these results to previous studies. The second section tracks numbers of immigrants, refugees and

Acknowledgments for information on the eight colleges with large ESL populations are as follows: Arthur Kramer, director of institutional research, Passaic County Community College, New Jersey; Nancy Soteriou, institutional research associate, and Dennis Brown, dean, communications division, El Paso Community College; Michael Kritikos, registrar, Harry S. Truman College, Chicago; Marcia Belcher, research associate, and Barbara Echord, district dean of academic affairs, Miami–Dade Community College; Stuart Wilcox, associate dean of admissions and records, Pasadena City College; Sam Hirsch, dean of educational support services, Community College of Philadelphia; and Frank Plucker, division dean of language arts, Yuba College, Marysville, California.

asylees, and foreign student entrants into the United States between 1940 and 1990. The final section looks at the implications for community colleges in the future given the continuing growth in ESL populations throughout the country.

Results of the 1991 National Curriculum Study

In the first CSCC curriculum study conducted in 1975, ESL was coded as a sub-subject under the larger subject area of foreign languages, which was part of the discipline of humanities. For comparison purposes, we have kept ESL under the foreign language coding category for all subsequent CSCC curriculum studies, including this latest 1991 study. Noncredit ESL courses were not tallied, since the focus of the CSCC study was on the liberal arts credit portion of the community college curriculum. The placement of ESL credit courses in the community college liberal arts curriculum is by no means standardized, and the departmental home of ESL varies considerably from college to college. Sometimes ESL is located in language arts departments which can include English, Basic Skills, ESL, speech, and foreign languages; sometimes it occupies a place in the college as its own fiefdom under "ESL and Bilingual Education"; and sometimes it is subsumed under as many as three different departments, as at Pasadena City College, depending on the skills being taught and whether the courses carry institutional credit.

The following tables attest to the growth in ESL as part of the community college liberal arts curriculum between 1975 and 1991. Table 5.1 charts the 14 percent increase in the number of colleges that offered any ESL sections over a sixteen-year span. For comparison purposes, it may be noted that while 40 percent of community colleges in the sample for 1991 reported offering ESL credit courses, 77 percent of the same 164 colleges reported offering Spanish classes and 63 percent reported French course offerings.

An examination of the role of foreign languages, which includes ESL, shows that from 1977 to 1991 foreign languages grew slightly more than 15 percent as part of the total humanities curriculum. Furthermore, foreign languages grew from 5 percent to 8.5 percent of the total liberal arts curriculum in the five years between 1986 and 1991. This increase in the percentage of foreign language sections offered is due solely to the rise in ESL. In 1983 ESL

Table 5.1. Percentage of Community Colleges Offering ESL During Spring Term in Each Year

1975	1977	1983	1986	1991
(n = 156)	(n = 178)	(n = 173)	(n = 95)	(n = 164)
26%	33%	27%	38%	40%

accounted for only 30 percent of the foreign language sections offered; by 1986 that percentage had jumped to 43 percent, and by 1991 had further increased to 51 percent. Thus, even though only 40 percent of the colleges in the sample offered ESL classes (as shown in Table 5.1) ESL sections accounted for over half (51 percent) of all foreign language sections tallied (see Table 5.2).

Data gathered in the 1991 CSCC curriculum study also included second-census or end-of-term enrollment figures for a random sample of course sections. Enrollment and average class size figures were calculated for both foreign languages and ESL, based on the sample of 164 colleges and extrapolated to the population of 1,250 U.S. community colleges. These figures are duplicated headcounts and represent students enrolled in an individual class. ESL accounted for 236,000 of the 460,700 total foreign language enrollment.

The increase shown in ESL as part of the liberal arts curriculum was the largest of any of the subject areas in the 1991 curriculum study. From where are these students coming? Can we expect the increase to continue? What are their backgrounds and what impact will they have on community colleges?

National Statistics on Limited English Proficient Adults, Immigrants, Refugees, and Foreign Students

Information on the extent of the potential demand for ESL courses must be collected from a number of different sources. The demand for ESL comes from different population sectors and a compilation of information from several national databases and reports, tracking the arrival of immigrants, refugees, asylees, and foreign students into this country since 1940, can yield a composite picture.

Table 5.2. **Percentage of Foreign Language Class Sections Within Each Subject Area During Spring Term**

Subject	1983	1986	1991
ESL	30%	43%	51%
Spanish	35	29	24
French	18	15	10
Asian	N.A.	N.A.	5
German	10	7	4
Other	3	2	3
Italian	2	3	2
Russian	< 1	1	< 1
Classics	< 1	< 1	< 1

Note: Due to rounding, totals may equal more than 100%.

The 1980 and 1990 Censuses provide data on the limited English proficient (LEP) adult population, while the 1990 *Statistical Yearbook of the Immigration and Naturalization Service* contains the most up-to-date information on figures for immigrants, refugees and asylees, and foreign students entering the country. In synthesizing the information from these sources, a picture of the rising numbers of ESL students into the country emerges. Statistics concerning populations which might avail themselves of ESL classes in U.S. community colleges are described below.

The Limited English Proficient Population. Because both the 1980 and the 1990 censuses recorded languages spoken at home by age, citizenship, sex, and ability to speak English, data from these two censuses can be compared to investigate any changes in the LEP population. In censuses prior to 1980, the wording of the question on current language was "mother tongue" and is not directly comparable to information on language for the 1980 and 1990 censuses. Also, for the first time ever in a U.S. census, the 1990 Census attempted to calculate the degree of linguistic isolation of members of surveyed households.

In 1980, 8.8 percent of citizens 18 years of age or over reported speaking a language other than English at home. For all age groups, over 23 million reported speaking a language other than English, equaling 10.9 percent of the total population. In addition, 2 percent of the population that spoke English reported that they did not speak English well or did not speak it at all (U.S. Bureau of the Census, 1980, Table 256). In comparison, data from the 1990 Census revealed that 13.79 percent of the population age 18 and over spoke a language other than English at home. For all age groups, close to 32 million reported speaking a language other than English at home, or 13.82 percent of the total population, an increase of almost 9 million persons between 1980 and 1990. Not all of these 32 million persons, however, would be potential candidates for community college ESL classes. Those over 18 who spoke a language other than English and who indicated that they spoke English not well or not at all numbered 5,764,638, or 3.11 percent. Census data between 1980 and 1990 show that the LEP proportion of the population has grown, both in terms of actual number of respondents and in overall percentages of LEP persons.

Because the above census questions do not ask whether respondents were fully bilingual, or whether a language other than English was the main or dominant language used at home, these percentages yield only rough estimates of the extent of limited English proficiency. A new category of questions in the 1990 Census, however, attempted to measure the degree of *linguistic isolation,* a measure which may be a more accurate assessment of limited English proficiency. Linguistic isolation is defined as "A household in which no person age 14 years or over speaks only English and no person age 14 years or over who speaks a language other than English speaks English 'very well' is classified as 'linguistically isolated.' All the members of a linguistically isolated household are tabulated as linguistically isolated, including members under age 14 years who may speak only English" (U.S. Bureau of the Census, 1990).

Of the more than 77,600,000 households surveyed in the 1990 Census, almost three million (2,936,596) reported linguistic isolation. Slightly over three percent of the U.S. households, then, are considered linguistically isolated. Of the population of interest to community colleges, a similar percentage (3.3 percent) of those ages 18 to 64 are considered to belong to linguistically isolated households. The actual number of LEP persons between the ages of 18 and 64 who belong to linguistically isolated households is estimated to be close to 5 million (4,968,023).

Immigrant and Refugee and Asylee Populations. Immigration to the United States has increased steadily since the mid-1940s. The 1990 *Statistical Yearbook of the Immigration and Naturalization Service* reports that while today's immigration figures are still much below that of 1900–1910 when immigration averaged around 880,000 persons annually, the numbers have climbed steadily since 1945. During the decade between 1981 and 1990, that average number was 733,800—the closest the United States has yet come to the all-time high averages of the first decade of this century. Immigration in the United States jumped dramatically between 1988 and 1989—from 643,025 in 1988 to 1,090,924 in 1989. In 1990, the last year for which national statistics are publicly available, immigration was the highest it has been in U.S. history—1,536,483. This large increase is due mainly to the Immigration Reform and Control Act (IRCA) of 1986, discussed below. Excluding immigrants adjusting under the special conditions of the IRCA, immigration increased by only 7.2 percent between 1989 and 1990 (INS, 1991). Table 5.3 charts both immigration and refugee and asylee[1] admissions to the United States by total numbers admitted for each decade since 1940.

Portés and Rumbaut (1990) report figures shown in Table 5.4 for both immigrant and native-born limited English proficient populations and show an increase in the percentage of the immigrant population arriving after 1970 that spoke a language other than English at home.

**Table 5.3. Immigrant, Refugee, and Asylee Admissions
to the United States, 1941–1990**

Year	Immigrants	Refugees/Asylees
1941–50[a]	1,035,039	213,347
1951–60	2,515,479	492,371
1961–70	3,321,677	212,843
1971–80	4,493,314	539,447
1981–90	7,338,062	1,013,620

[a] Refugee figures are available only for the years 1946–1950 for the decade of the 1940s.

Source: U.S. Immigration and Natualization Service, 1991, pp. 47, 108.

Table 5.4. Home Language of Immigrants and Native-Born Americans

	English Only (%)	Other than English (%)
Total post-1970 immigrants	16.3	83.7
Total pre-1970 immigrants	38.3	61.7
Total native born	93.2	6.8

Source: Portés and Rumbaut, 1990, pp. 200–201.

Immigrants are more likely to settle in large urban areas, and as a result urban community colleges experience greater growth in the pool of potential ESL students than do community colleges in less-populated parts of the country. An illustration of the growth experienced in two urban community college districts in California portrays the potential impact of immigration upon urban districts. Data from the 1980 and 1990 censuses chart the tremendous growth in the Asian and Pacific Islander and Hispanic-origin populations in both Los Angeles and Orange Counties. In Los Angeles County, the Hispanic-origin population grew from 27.6 percent of the total population to 37.8 percent, a 62.2 percent increase within ten years, while the Asian and Pacific Islander population grew from 6.1 percent in 1980 to 10.8 percent of the total population in 1990, an increase of 109.6 percent. In Orange County, the growth rate was just as impressive, with the Hispanic-origin population jumping from 14.8 percent to 23.4 percent of the county's total population, a 97.3 percent increase, and the Asian and Pacific Islander population expanding from 4.8 percent to 10.3 percent of the county's total population, a 166.2 percent increase (Turner and Allen, 1990). While these examples from California are some of the most extreme in the country, other urban community colleges throughout the United States are also affected by the growth in U.S. immigration.

In estimating the effects of increasing immigration to the United States on community colleges' ESL programs, a consideration of legislation mandating language education is essential. One such piece of legislation is the Immigration Reform and Control Act of 1986, the so-called Amnesty Act. The purpose of the IRCA was to halt the flow of illegal immigrants between the Mexican–U.S. border and to provide a way in which illegal immigrants who had already spent substantial amounts of time in the United States might become part of mainstream America. In order to push this act through Congress, an education requirement that mandated 40 hours of instruction in English, U.S. history and civics was added (Huss, 1990).

The impact of immigration upon schools, including community colleges, across the United States that provide English, history, and civics courses has been enormous. In 1990 alone, 880,372 aliens were admitted under provisions of the IRCA of 1986—out of a record total of 1,536,483 aliens or 57.3

percent of the total immigration to the United States for that year (INS, 1991). The fact that 57 percent of U.S. immigration in 1990 was admitted under the proviso of an educational requirement that mandated English language training is all the more noteworthy if we consider that since the IRCA has been in effect, 3 million undocumented aliens applied for temporary residency, and thus they too required English, U.S. history, and civics classes (Huss, 1990). As one way of fulfilling the 40-hour education requirement, eligible legalized aliens could show proof of full-time attendance for one complete year at a state-approved institution, a category which includes community colleges.

Foreign Student Population. Although the number of foreign students entering the United States affects the community colleges to a lesser degree than four-year institutions, the steady increase in those numbers has been felt in community college enrollment admission policies. More foreign students are studying in the United States than in any other country in the world (Baldwin, 1991). Using data from the Institute of International Education (IIE), the *Chronicle of Higher Education* published an article in November 1992 stating that foreign enrollment at U.S. colleges and universities reached an all-time high of 419,585 for that academic year (Watkins, 1992). A year later, in the December 1, 1993 issue, the *Chronicle* reported a new record high of 438,618 foreign students enrolled in U.S. colleges and universities, a 4.5 percent increase over 1991–1992, (Desruisseaux, 1993). From 1949/50 to 1985/86, foreign student enrollment, like immigration, has risen steadily. The figures from the *Chronicle* articles, which are based on IIE data, are included with additional figures from the IIE (Zikopoulos, 1988) and presented in Table 5.5.

Of the foreign students who studied in the United States in 1992–1993, 13 percent (57,150) attended two-year colleges. At a few community colleges, the percentage of the foreign student population is significant. At Santa Monica College foreign students comprise 8.7 percent of the total student population (Desruisseaux, 1993).

Table 5.5. Foreign Student Enrollment in the United States, 1949–1992

Year	Foreign Student Enrollment
1949/50	26,433
1959/60	48,486
1969/70	134,959
1979/80	286,340
1985/86	343,780
1991/92	419,585
1992/93	438,618

Source: Zikopoulos, 1988, p. 22; Watkins, 1992, p. A28; Desruisseaux, 1993, p A42–43.

Table 5.5 documents the steady increase in foreign student enrollment at U.S. institutions of higher education. In an era of swelling enrollment in all sectors of higher education, community colleges may soon have to decide—and indeed, a few have already decided—whether they can afford to admit foreign students into their programs and whether foreign student admissions adversely affect U.S. student opportunities for higher education.

If we use data from all the above sources to calculate the total pool of ESL students who might have elected to enroll in community college ESL classes during 1990–1991, a rough estimate of 5,902,395 is reached (4,968,023 linguistically isolated U.S. citizens between the ages of 18 and 64, plus an estimated 13 percent of the total foreign student population for 1990–1991, and 880,372 aliens admitted under provision of the IRCA, which required instruction in English as a condition for legalization). While only a percentage of the estimated nearly 6 million potential ESL candidates will actually take an ESL class at a community college, the pool is substantial and growing.

As illustrated above, the LEP, immigrant, refugee and asylee, and foreign student populations have all increased in the United States over the past decade. With that increase arises a concomitant increase in the demand for ESL. It appears likely that the nation's community colleges will continue to grapple with the problem of how best to deliver educational services to a growing ESL population.

Participants in the 1991 National Curriculum Study with Large ESL Programs

Eight community colleges from the Spring 1991 CSCC curriculum study offered high numbers of ESL sections. Contact persons at each of the community colleges were telephoned in order to solicit information concerning their ESL populations. Table 5.6 lists these eight colleges and provides the number of ESL sections offered and the percentage of ESL as part of the total liberal arts curriculum.

The ESL Community College Population. In order to determine ESL student enrollment in the eight programs listed above, a look at how colleges define ESL students and where they put them is needed, since ESL students are often reported differently among institutions. Some colleges separate students by credit and noncredit program enrollment. Other colleges have beginning ESL classes for students who know little or no English. Still other colleges pass these beginning ESL students over to the district Adult Basic Education programs. Therefore, enrollment figures for ESL students can vary from institution to institution depending on how a particular community college structures its ESL programming. All of the eight programs studied reported over 1,000 ESL students.

Table 5.6. 1991 Curriculum Study Participants
Reporting Large ESL Programs

College	Number of ESL Sections[a]	ESL as Percentage of Total Liberal Arts
El Paso Community College (TX)	429	26.0%
Harry S. Truman College (Chicago, IL)	243	42.2
Passaic County Community College (Paterson, NJ)	160	38.6
Miami-Dade Community College (South Campus only)	152	9.7
San Jose City College (CA)	89	16.6
Community College of Philadelphia	83	6.4
Pasadena City College (CA)	71	5.7
Yuba College (Marysville, CA)	70	12.4

[a] Tally does not include laboratory classes or tutorial sessions. Sections counted were those with a designated meeting time and place on the course schedule.

A look at 1991 ESL student enrollment figures at four of the colleges creates a better picture of the impact of ESL on community colleges. Miami–Dade estimated 10,000 ESL students on all four of its campuses, although only the South Campus was included in the 1991 CSCC curriculum study. An estimated 4,000 students took ESL at Pasadena City College, with between 1,800 and 1,900 enrolled in ESL for credit. At Harry S. Truman College in Chicago, Illinois, approximately 2,500 students took ESL classes. And at El Paso Community College, ESL accounted for 5,225 hours of instruction in the fall of 1991; full-time ESL students alone numbered 1,045.

The linguistic and educational backgrounds of these students varied from college to college and affected the type of ESL programs the college offered. At the Community College of Philadelphia, ESL students came from 56 different countries. Twenty-one percent of the students were Vietnamese, 16.7 percent were Spanish-speaking, and 14 percent were Russian. At Harry S. Truman College in Chicago, 60 percent (1,500 out of 2,500) were Russian. Seventy percent of El Paso Community College's population was Hispanic, although not all took ESL classes. The Gujarati-speaking population at Passaic County Community College in New Jersey was second only to the Spanish-speaking ESL population at the college. Thirty-six percent of Pasadena City's ESL students spoke some dialect of Chinese as their first language. And at Yuba College, the Hmong were only slightly behind Spanish-speaking ESL students as the largest language group at that college.

The foreign student population also varied from college to college in the study. At the Community College of Philadelphia, no foreign students were admitted. Given funding levels, the college leadership felt that the commitment should be to nonforeign students and therefore instituted a policy of nonacceptance of I-20 (foreign student) visas. Passaic County Community

College, El Paso Community College, and Truman College all reported between 150 and 200 foreign students studying on their campuses. At Miami–Dade, the philosophy toward foreign students is one of open admission. The Miami–Dade course catalog states that "Although no International students will be denied admission because of their TOEFL score, submission of a TOEFL score is required to complete the admissions process" (Miami–Dade Community College 1991 course catalog, p. 23). This open admissions policy is reflected in the fact that Miami–Dade's four campuses enrolled 1,924 international students (a figure which excluded refugee and asylee students) in Fall Term 1991–1992, a higher number than any other community college in the country (Almanac of the *Chronicle of Higher Education*, 1993).

Another category of ESL students on community college campuses is due to the Immigration Reform and Control Act, or the "Amnesty Act," passed in 1986. Some community colleges reported huge increases in ESL student enrollments once the act went into effect, while at other colleges the Amnesty Act students were handled in evening classes through the Adult Basic Education program. At Pasadena City College, an estimated 12,300 hours of instruction were generated in the noncredit ESL program by Amnesty Act students in the 1990–1991 academic year. Funding for the IRCA ran out in 1993 and critics of the act report that the educational requirement attached to it has been a failure. One report noted that community colleges in California were only prepared to provide courses to fulfill the 40-hour educational requirement to approximately 25 percent of the eligible applicants (Scott-Skillman and Saeed, 1991). Clearly, the demand for ESL classes created by the IRCA was much greater than what community colleges could deliver.

One final note concerning the background of ESL student populations is that their resources vary as greatly as their language backgrounds. And as their resources vary, so do their educational requirements. Pasadena City College reports that part of its ESL population is students who are repatriating to the United States and who come from well-to-do backgrounds. These students no doubt require less financial assistance from the college and can provide for much of their own postsecondary educational needs. In contrast, 95 percent of the ESL students at El Paso Community College receive financial assistance through Pell grants. The educational and socio-economic backgrounds of ESL students are factors in shaping the ESL curriculum offered by an individual college. The resources of the college are another factor. ESL students who require either academic or financial assistance can place an added burden upon already-strained community college budgets, with the result that colleges may be hard-pressed to provide necessary services to this population. Federal assistance is available to offset at least some of the financial need, but college administrations need to plan carefully to obtain adequate assistance.

ESL Enrollment Projections. Three of the community colleges with large ESL populations reported a stabilizing trend concerning projections for future enrollment. The 1991–1992 academic year was the first year that the ESL population at El Paso Community College stabilized. This stabilization may be due in part to the newly implemented Congressional "ability to benefit from education" requirement that has resulted in a restriction of the number of ESL students who qualify for financial aid at El Paso. Recently, however, college officials are anticipating increased demand for ESL due in part to the passage of NAFTA. Two other community colleges are planning a shift in the provision of the lowest level of ESL from the regular college program to the Adult Basic Education program and added that this change may stabilize their ESL programs within the regular liberal arts program.

Officials at three of the eight colleges in the study reported an expected increase in ESL enrollment, with the Community College of Philadelphia anticipating a tremendous increase, especially in Russian and Asian-born populations. Political factors in nearby countries, such as Nicaragua and Cuba, and in not-so-nearby countries, such as those in Eastern Europe, influence the numbers of ESL students who eventually enter community college programs. Additional consequences of the 1986 Amnesty Act may also affect ESL student enrollment in community colleges, as close relatives of recent amnesty applicants also immigrate to the United States. Nearly 70 percent of Amnesty Act recipients are male and it is likely that they will be joined by their immediate families (Daniels, 1990).

Statistics on immigrants, refugees, and asylees to the United States, as well as an increasing foreign student population, point to a continuing increase in the number of ESL students in U.S. community college classrooms. Because no evidence exists for any imminent decline in the demand for ESL, many community colleges will need to continue to provide large numbers of ESL sections as the demand for these courses goes unabated.

Implications for Policy and Planning

The implications for community colleges regarding the growth in ESL are enormous. Officials in community colleges where large numbers of ESL students are enrolled cite varied concerns—from budgets to special counseling services to college mission. Three of the main concerns expressed by community college officials are described below.

Perhaps the most important concern is that of the college's mission. Is the most important mission of a community college to be a "college" and thus to focus upon transfer and occupational-technical missions, or is it to address the needs of the community and provide more ESL classes? Is it necessary to choose between missions? What is the community college's community? If a large ESL population is housed within an immediate five-mile radius of the campus, should the concerns of these students outweigh the concerns of students county- or district-wide? Are "being a college" and "teaching ESL"

mutually exclusive concepts—especially if ESL courses are academically vigorous? If ESL students are occupying classrooms on many of today's crowded
community college campuses, it may mean that classrooms are not available
for students in other programs. If, for example, student demand for science
and psychology as well as ESL is increasing, to which department is classroom
space allocated? Because many community colleges are committed to the ideal
of open access and open enrollments, this issue goes to the heart of the college's mission.

Concomitant with mission is the structure of the ESL program, including
the departmental home of ESL. Community colleges which house ESL in several departments—credit courses as well as noncredit—may need to investigate whether their ESL population is best served through this arrangement.
Whereas colleges may develop different ESL delivery patterns to capitalize
upon the often diverse funding streams available for ESL, housing ESL in different campus departments may not be the best course in terms of services
delivered to ESL students and overall use of college resources. Writing in 1978,
Martorana noted just such potential fragmentation when funding sources follow the student (Martorana, 1978). This concept of fragmented delivery systems can be applied to ESL, for if federal and state policies are an important
means of gaining money for community college ESL programs, then separate
services (testing, counseling, certification, instruction) may be the result.

A second major concern expressed by community college officials was the
ability of ESL students to perform well linguistically in regular content-area
classrooms once they have finished their ESL program. Community college faculty sometimes complain that ESL students cannot handle content courses in
English. This problem is further exacerbated when ESL students enroll in content-area classes before they have finished their ESL coursework. Because ESL
classes generally do not carry degree or certificate credits, students may not
want to waste their time in ESL classes. Typically, however, no policy exists
which mandates that students take sufficient English language classes before
enrolling in regular program classes. Faculty, therefore, have a more difficult
task when faced with ESL students whose language proficiency levels prevent
them from understanding content-area course material.

The third concern regards the development and sequencing of courses to
keep ESL student motivation high. As stated above, ESL students may perceive
ESL classes as a waste of time (and financial aid monies) and see little reason
to delay entry into regular content-area classes. Should these students be
allowed to take a certain number of content-area courses even though their
language skills may be weak in order to keep their motivation for further education high? Or should these students be prevented from continuing coursework in content areas until their English is strong enough for them to pass a
basic skills test? If commitment to equity and open access are values the community college holds, then how far should community colleges go in provid-

ing opportunities for ESL students who may start their postsecondary education with linguistic and sometimes educational disadvantages?

One response to both the second and third concerns expressed above was developed by the Community College of Philadelphia through their "transitional program." ESL students who have reached a certain level of English language proficiency can take classes that address both ESL and content-area learning. An example of a transitional program course would be a course for advanced ESL readers taught in English by a faculty member of the psychology department. Students receive psychology credit for the class. Class size is kept low so that the instructor has time to work on students' language skills as well as content-area skills. Testing and placement are features of this ESL program, and special one-on-one counseling for ESL students is also built into the system. At registration, a "hold" is put on an ESL student's card to prevent the student from changing ESL courses to content-area courses. Faculty and administrators at the Community College of Philadelphia worked together to provide an appropriate curriculum that would keep ESL student motivation high and still teach ESL and any necessary content-area skills. College officials state that students who go through ESL and transfer to the regular college program do well. In general, they have much higher retention and persistence rates than the general student population—as much as 20 percent retention increases over other students, although ESL student GPAs may not be as high as those of students who enter academic programs already proficient in English.

Conclusion

Given the statistics on projections of immigrant, refugee, and asylee entrants to the United States, as well as on continuing foreign student enrollment, the demand for ESL is not going to go away. As the results of the 1991 CSCC curriculum study have shown, ESL has increased tremendously since 1975 and shows no signs of abating within the near future. Community colleges will need to continue to meet the challenge of developing suitable education for their ESL students. Setting clear definitions of "mission" and "community" is a first step in establishing policies and designing programs which fit local circumstances. Spending the requisite time and effort to establish a consistent, coherent policy toward ESL students—preferably district-wide—is also essential. And sharing the excellent ways in which community colleges across the United States are already meeting the educational challenges of large numbers of ESL students through innovative programs and curriculum is another.

Notes

1. The Refugee Act of 1980 defines a refugee as "any person outside his or her country of nationality who is unable or unwilling to return to that country because of persecution or a well-

founded fear of persecution" (U.S. Immigration and Naturalization Service, 1991, p. 96). An asylee is any person claiming asylum while on American soil or at an American embassy.

References

Baldwin, A. "International Student Profile." Research Report No. 91–11R. Office of Institutional Research, Miami–Dade Community College, 1991.

Chronicle of Higher Education Almanac. Washington, D.C.: Chronicle of Higher Education, 1993.

Daniels, R. Coming to America. New York: HarperCollins, 1991.

Desruisseaux, P. "A Foreign-Student Record." Chronicle of Higher Education, Dec. 1, 1993, pp. A42–43.

Huss, S. "The Education Requirement of the U.S. Immigration Reform and Control Act of 1986: A Case Study of Ineffective Language Planning." Language Problems and Language Planning, 1990, 14 (2), 142–161.

Martorana, S. V. "Shifting Patterns of Financial Support." In R. L. Alfred (ed.), Coping with Reduced Resources. New Directions for Community Colleges, no. 22. San Francisco: Jossey-Bass, 1978.

Portés, A., and Rumbaut, R. G. Immigrant America: A Portrait. Berkeley: University of California Press, 1990.

Scott-Skillman, T., and Saeed, A. M. "Beyond Amnesty: Programs and Services for the New Californians." 1991. (ED 335 083)

Turner, E., and Allen, J. P. An Atlas of Population Patterns in Metropolitan Los Angeles and Orange Counties, 1990. Northridge: Department of Geography, California State University, Northridge, 1990.

U.S. Bureau of the Census. 1980 Census of Population, Vol. 1: Characteristics of the Population. (Chapter 3: Detailed Population Characteristics. Part 1. United States Summary Section A: United States Tables 253–310.) Washington, D.C.: U.S. Government Printing Office, 1980.

U.S. Bureau of the Census. 1990 Census of Population. U.S. Summary Data, Summary Tape File 3C, Tables P28–30. Washington, D.C.: U.S. Government Printing Office, 1990a.

U.S. Bureau of the Census. 1990 Census of Population and Housing—Guide. Washington, D.C.: U.S. Government Printing Office, 1990b.

U.S. Government. The President's Comprehensive Triennial Report on Immigration, 1989. Washington, D.C.: U.S. Government Printing Office, 1989.

U.S. Immigration and Naturalization Service. Statistical Yearbook of the U.S. Immigration and Naturalization Service, 1990. Washington, D.C.: U.S. Government Printing Office, 1991.

Watkins, B. T. "Foreign Enrollment at U.S. Colleges and Universities Totaled 419,585 in 1991–92, An All-Time High." Chronicle of Higher Education, Nov. 25, 1992, p. A28.

Zikopoulos, M. (ed.) Profiles: Detailed Analyses of the Foreign Student Population. New York: Institute of International Education, 1988.

JAN M. IGNASH is a research assistant at the Center for the Study of Community Colleges and a doctoral candidate in higher education at the University of California, Los Angeles.

Why do ethnic studies courses exist? To what extent are they offered? Do ethnic studies course offerings vary with institutional characteristics?

What Influences Community College Ethnic Studies Course Offerings?

Susan Sean Swayze

College student protest brought ethnic studies courses into the college curriculum in the late sixties and early seventies. Since then, ethnic studies coursework has been integrated into the liberal arts curriculum. The need for ethnic studies courses has not abated. In fact, there is great need for them now; our society is becoming increasingly more diverse and ethnic studies courses may aid in greater interaction and understanding among the various ethnic segments of American society. This chapter explores ethnic studies course offerings in community colleges. It includes descriptions of the variance in ethnic studies course offerings by institutional characteristics such as nonwhite enrollment, enrollment size, and liberal arts course offerings.

Ethnic studies courses are those that focus on the experience of groups that are "differentiated from the dominant group population by race, nationality, language, religion, culture, and tradition who/which have suffered and do suffer, in the United States, unequal treatment, prejudice, and discrimination in our society"—African Americans, Latinos, Asian Americans, and Native Americans (Chavez, 1984, p. 33). Ethnic studies courses "provide students an opportunity to examine the social, historical, cultural, political, and economic experiences and backgrounds of racial-ethnic minority groups in the United States" and "assist in developing, among students, an awareness, understanding, and appreciation for the varied ethnic-racial minority groups in our multicultural community in an effort to achieve a more equal and just society" (Chavez, 1984, pp. 32-33).

Levine and Cureton (1992) conducted a study of 196 two-year and four-year institutions and found that many colleges and universities offer ethnic studies courses; the results are shown in Table 6.1.

Table 6.1. Percentage of U.S. Colleges and Universities Offering Ethnic Studies Courses

Type of Ethnic Studies Course	All Institutions	Two-Year Colleges
African-American Studies	43%	31%
Asian-American Studies	35	25
Hispanic-American Studies	37	29
Native-American Studies	33	20

Source: Levine and Cureton, 1992.

Their data show that at least a third of all institutions offer courses in ethnic studies. The proportion decreases, however, when two-year colleges are analyzed alone. The Center for the Study of Community Colleges (CSCC) has examined the liberal arts curriculum since 1975. They reported that 22 percent of all community colleges offered ethnic studies courses in 1975, 10 percent in 1983, and 15 percent in 1991. These findings are in contrast to Levine and Cureton's study. Such a contrast may be the result of the strict coding used by the CSCC. Only truly interdisciplinary ethnic studies courses were coded as ethnic studies courses. An example of an interdisciplinary ethnic studies course is "Black Americans," a course that includes historical, economic, and sociological discussions of African Americans. A course that focuses on only one disciplinary aspect of an ethnic studies topic, such as the Sociology of Asian Americans, would be coded as a sociology course, not an ethnic studies course. Hence, there is a discrepancy between the CSCC and Levine and Cureton studies.

Peterson and Cepeda (1985) studied California community colleges and concluded that ethnic studies course offerings were extensive in the state. They reported that of the 107 California community colleges, 21 had an ethnic studies requirement for an associate degree, 48 offered'an associate degree in ethnic studies, and 6 offered nondegree certificate programs. They found 807 different ethnic studies courses offered in 34 instructional areas. The largest instructional areas with courses that focus on ethnic-racial minorities were:

Subject Area	Number of Ethnic Studies Courses
History	205 (25%)
Social sciences/sociology	78 (10%)
Mexican-American/Chicano studies	70 (9%)
Ethnic/multicultural studies	69 (9%)
African-American/black studies	56 (7%)
English/literature	50 (6%)

Although Peterson and Cepeda examined only California community colleges, the fact that two single-discipline instructional areas, history and social sciences/sociology, led the interdisciplinary instructional areas of Mexican-American/Chicano studies, ethnic/multicultural studies, and African-American/black studies is important.

Because the CSCC 1991 curriculum study used a conservative coding scheme that counted only interdisciplinary ethnic studies courses, I believe the CSCC study presents an underestimation of ethnic studies course offerings in the nation's community colleges. To address this undercount, I reexamined the data from the CSCC curriculum study and this time counted all courses that focused on American ethnic minorities as ethnic studies courses—whether the courses were taught from an interdisciplinary perspective or a single-disciplinary perspective. This inclusion is important in order to provide a more accurate picture of ethnic studies course offerings.

Further analysis of the various disciplines was conducted to find the ethnic emphases within other disciplines. This yielded an additional nine subject areas likely to house single-disciplinary ethnic studies courses: art history appreciation—specialized culture; cultural anthropology—other specialized; literature—group; anthropology—specialized culture; sociology—sociology of particular groups; cultural anthropology—American Indian; history—special groups; anthropology—Indian and Native American; and interdisciplinary sociology—special groups.

Counting these courses increased the number of community colleges offering courses with an ethnic studies emphasis to 68 (41 percent) of the total 164 colleges. This number is a considerable increase over the 14 colleges that offered interdisciplinary ethnic studies courses. In addition, all of the 14 colleges that offered interdisciplinary ethnic studies courses also offered at least one discipline-specific ethnic studies course. Single-discipline ethnic studies course offerings were distributed as follows:

Course Type	Number of Colleges
Cultural anthropology: American Indian	5
Anthropology: Native American	3
Cultural anthropology: specialized ethnic	3
History of special groups	52
Group literature	31
Anthropology: special group	3
Interdisciplinary sociology	1
Sociology of special groups	29
Art history or art appreciation: special group	12

Twenty-seven colleges offered ethnic studies courses in only one coding category; seventeen colleges in two coding categories; seventeen colleges in three coding categories; and seven colleges offered ethnic studies courses in four coding categories. A few of the titles found in these catalogs are included here for illustration: Asian-American Communities, Minority Economic Survival, Psychology of African Americans, Racism in America, Introduction to Native American Literature, Modern Black Political Thought, Puerto Rican Experiences in the Urban United States, Ethnic Groups in American Life, Asian-American History, Sociology of African Americans, American Indian History and Culture, Black Women, Black Men, African-American Writing, and The Puerto Rican Family.

As shown by the titles of courses, there is a wide variety of ethnic studies courses offered by community colleges.

Ethnic Enrollment

Relative to four-year college enrollment, American ethnic groups are highly concentrated in community colleges. The data presented in "Where America goes to college" (American Association of Community and Junior Colleges, 1990, p. 1) shows that "minorities are more likely to attend community, technical, and junior colleges than Caucasians." Community colleges enroll "36 percent of the nation's Caucasian college students, . . . 57 percent of Native American college students, 55 percent of Hispanic college students, 43 percent of African-American college students, and 41 percent of Asian college students" (American Association of Community and Junior Colleges, 1990, p. 1). Do ethnic studies course offerings vary by the ethnic composition of the institution? Data detailing community college student ethnicity were available for 156 of the total 164 colleges. Most of the colleges, 109 of the 156, had at least 40 percent nonwhite (African-American, Asian-American, Latino, and Native American) enrollment. Of these 109, 65 did not offer an ethnic studies course. The distributions of ethnic studies course offerings by nonwhite enrollment are shown in Table 6.2.

Thus the likelihood of ethnic studies course offerings varies by the percent of nonwhite student enrollment. Colleges with less than 40 percent

Table 6.2. Community College Nonwhite Enrollment and Number of Ethnic Studies Courses

Number of Ethnic Studies Courses Offered	Percent Nonwhite Enrollment				
	< 20% (n = 68)	20–39% (n = 41)	40–59% (n = 24)	60–79% (n = 15)	> 79% (n = 8)
0	41 (60%)	24 (59%)	12 (50%)	7 (47%)	4 (50%)
1–5	15	9	6	3	2
6–15	11	6	3	3	1
16–25	1	2	1	2	0
26–40	0	0	2	0	1

Note: N = 156

nonwhite enrollment are less likely to offer an ethnic studies course than colleges with at least 40 percent nonwhite enrollment. Of the colleges with less than 40 percent nonwhite enrollment (109), the number of colleges with no ethnic studies courses (65) was greater than the number of colleges with ethnic studies courses (44). Of the colleges with at least 40 percent nonwhite enrollment (47), the number of colleges with no ethnic studies courses (23) was equal to the number of colleges with ethnic studies courses (24). Although the availability of ethnic studies courses increases as non-white enrollment increases, the number of ethnic studies course offerings does not seem to follow the same pattern. Higher nonwhite student enrollment does not necessarily lead to a larger number of ethnic studies course offerings. Four colleges in the database had at least 90 percent nonwhite enrollment but three of the four offered either one or no ethnic studies courses while the fourth had 36 such courses. Having at least 90 percent nonwhite enrollment does not guarantee that ethnic studies courses are offered. Additionally, where ethnic studies courses are offered, one course may be offered or 36 courses may be offered.

To summarize, the ethnic composition of a college is more likely to affect whether any ethnic studies courses are offered, not the number of courses offered.

Size of College

Do ethnic studies courses vary by college size? A college is considered small if it enrolls less than 1,500 students, medium if it enrolls between 1,500 and 6,000 students, and large if it enrolls more than 6,000 students. Table 6.3 shows a distribution of ethnic studies course offerings by the size of the college.

Thirty percent of small colleges, 42 percent of medium colleges, and 50 percent of large colleges offered ethnic studies courses. The likelihood of ethnic

Table 6.3. Community College Enrollment Size
and Number of Ethnic Studies Courses

Number of Ethnic Studies Courses Offered	Small (N = 47)	Medium (N = 59)	Large (N = 58)
0	33 (70%)	34 (58%)	29 (50%)
1–5	10	16	9
6–15	2	8	14
16–25	1	1	3
26–40	1	0	3

Note: N = 164. Small = less than 1,500 students; medium = 1,500–6,000 students; large = more than 6,000 students.

studies course offerings tends to vary by the size of the college—the larger the college, the more likely ethnic studies courses will be offered.

More ethnic studies courses are found in larger colleges than smaller ones, but do they vary by the number of liberal arts courses a college offers? Table 6.4 presents the number of ethnic studies courses by amount of liberal arts courses offered.

Table 6.4 does indicate that ethnic studies course offerings vary by liberal arts course offerings. To further illustrate this point, 18 of the 164 colleges were technical colleges; of these, 17 did not offer any ethnic studies courses. These colleges also had limited liberal arts course offerings. This finding makes sense; most ethnic studies courses were taught through a single-discipline perspective—history, literature, anthropology, or art history. These disciplines are all part of the liberal arts curriculum. Thus, it appears that the more liberal arts courses a community college offers, the greater the likelihood that the college will also offer one or more ethnic studies courses.

Conclusion

Interdisciplinary ethnic studies courses were taught in 8.5 percent of the nation's community colleges in 1991. However, 41 percent of community colleges taught ethnic studies courses with a single-discipline perspective. This figure is larger than previously found in CSCC studies and suggests that ethnic studies courses are more widespread than past figures indicated. Ethnic studies can be studied through a single-discipline perspective or an interdisciplinary one. It is important to note the various instructional areas in which ethnic studies courses are taught when one attempts to examine their presence in the college curriculum.

Ethnic studies course offerings tend to vary with community college composition and enrollment size. However, ethnic studies course offerings tend to vary in greater accordance with the number of liberal arts course offerings than

Table 6.4. Number of Ethnic Studies Courses by Amount of Liberal Arts Courses Offered

	Amount of Liberal Arts Curriculum		
Number of Ethnic Studies Courses Offered	Low (< 200) N = 73	Medium (200–500) N = 51	High (> 500) N = 40
0	64 (88%)	25 (49%)	7 (17.5%)
1 or more	9 (12%)	26 (51%)	33 (82.5%)

Note: Low = less than 200 students; medium = 200–500 students; high = more than 500 students.

with either ethnic composition or enrollment size. It appears that the larger the liberal arts course offerings of a college, the larger the ethnic studies course offerings at that college. The study of ethnic studies courses throughout the liberal arts curriculum is important for an accurate view of the availability of ethnic studies courses in our nation's colleges.

Suggestions for Future Research

The data presented here suggest variance in the offering of ethnic studies courses by nonwhite enrollment, enrollment size, and liberal arts course offerings. Because no correlational data are available, however, one cannot discuss levels of significance in regard to ethnic studies course offerings. Variables such as control (public/private) and location (urban/suburban/rural) need to be included in the examination of ethnic studies course offerings. The interactive effect of nonwhite enrollment, enrollment size, and liberal arts course offerings, as well as other relevant variables, needs to be examined in regard to the availability of ethnic studies course offerings. Further study of the availability of ethnic studies courses can be an important vehicle for ethnic understanding in our pluralistic society.

References

American Association of Community and Junior Colleges and the Association of Community College Trustees. "Where America Goes to College." Washington, D.C.: American Association of Community and Junior Colleges. 1990.

Chavez, M. "An Instructional Guide for Ethnic Studies at Evergreen Valley College." San Jose, Calif.: Evergreen Valley College, 1984. (ED 247 972)

Levine, A., and Cureton, J. "The Quiet Revolution: Eleven Facts about Multiculturalism and the Curriculum." *Change,* 1992, *24,* 25–29.

Peterson, A., and Cepeda, R. "Ethnic Studies, Policies, and Programs: A Response to Assembly Concurrent Resolution 71." Sacramento: Office of the Chancellor, California Community Colleges, 1985. (ED 252 258)

Stein, W. J. "Indian/Tribal Studies Programs in the Tribally Controlled Community." *Wicazo Sa Review,* Fall 1986, 2(2), 29–33. (ED 279 457)

SUSAN SEAN SWAYZE is a research assistant at the Center for the Study of Evaluation and a doctoral student in higher education at the University of California, Los Angeles.

What considerations are involved in deriving a valid, consistent method of estimating community college to four-year college transfer rates nationwide?

Analyzing Community College Student Transfer Rates

Arthur M. Cohen

This chapter examines the rate of student transfer from community colleges to universities in the United States. The data on which it is based are drawn from the Ford Foundation-funded Transfer Assembly project, coordinated by the Center for the Study of Community Colleges. Beginning in 1989, the project set out to define a valid way of calculating transfer rates that could be applied across the nation and to encourage colleges, universities, and state agencies to report data according to that definition. Its overall intent was to build a consistent way of estimating the community colleges' contribution to their students' progress toward the baccalaureate.

Caveats

From the outset the Transfer Assembly did not attempt to examine certain effects that were already well known. Among these:

• The transfer of students from community colleges to senior institutions is only one of the community colleges' major educational missions. Others include preparing students for job entry or career upgrading, teaching literacy and general education, and satisfying the students' personal interests. Measuring the colleges' transfer rates by no means tacitly elevates the transfer function above those others; it merely provides an indicator of institutional accomplishment in that one area.

Earlier versions of this chapter were presented at the annual meetings of the American Educational Research Association, Atlanta, April 14, 1993; the American Association of Community Colleges, Portland, Oregon, April 29, 1993; and the Association for Institutional Research, Chicago, May 19, 1993.

• The students who begin in a university are more likely to attain the baccalaureate than the students who begin in a community college; Astin (1993) and Orfield and Paul (1992), among others, have made that point repeatedly. The process is analogous to the likelihood of one's reaching a desired destination after having boarded a nonstop flight as compared with one who has to change planes along the way.

• Any definition or way of calculating transfer rates is imperfect because it excludes some pertinent data and because it is time bound. Much of the data about students' aspirations, particular curriculums that they follow, whether or not they attend full time, and the extent to which they are involved in campus life, either are not available or are compiled so inconsistently that they cannot be used in a broad-scale study. Furthermore, some students take five years, ten years, or longer to transfer (theoretically, students are potential transfers until they either show up at a university or die) but the data set must be cut off at some finite time.

With all of those caveats, what was the Center trying to do? The main purposes were to encourage the colleges to provide data on student flow in a consistent manner so that they can estimate the effects of interventions they make on behalf of this basic institutional function and to organize their student information systems so that they can respond readily to questions of student progress. For the external reviewer, the data collected in this fashion provide a base of national information that can be used to reconcile the conflicting claims that on the one hand the community college is a dead end for people seeking a baccalaureate or, on the other, that the community college is democracy's ultimate opportunity institution.

Definition

Many ways of estimating community college to university transfer rates have been used. Looking at the extremes, dividing the number of transfers in a given year by the total college enrollment yields a transfer rate of around 5 percent, whereas dividing the number of transfers by the number of students entering the college directly from high school, attending full time, declaring transfer intent, and receiving associate degrees may yield a rate near 85 percent. Obviously the definition of transfer rate is crucial.

The definition should be valid and readily understandable, and it should be based on data that are feasibly obtainable. In general, the number of students who enter the community college, subdivided according to certain criteria, must be divided into the number who subsequently matriculate at a four-year college or university. This yields a percentage, a transfer rate.

The question of which students to include in the cohort must be answered first. The definition should not use as its denominator all entrants to community colleges, because that figure includes students who already have degrees. It should not include only those students intending to transfer, because data on student intentions are unreliable. It should not include only the students just out of high school, because many students stop out of schooling and return to the community college when they are older. It should not be based on students who take only academic courses, because occupational education contributes to many transfers. It should not include only the full-time students, because part-time students account for two-thirds of the enrollment and many of the transfers. It should not include associate degree recipients only, since most of the transfers do so without obtaining a degree from the community college. It should not include sophomores only, because half the students transfer before obtaining as many as thirty units at the community college.

What *should* the definition include? The denominator should include only those students who take college-credit classes because most remedial and non-credit work is nontransferable. It should include students who complete some minimum number of units at the community college, those who have been enrolled long enough for the college staff to have a chance to work with them. It should allow at least a four-year span between community college entrance and transfer because few students matriculate and then move on within only a couple of years. And it should be based on data that are available from student records at the colleges and at the universities or the state system office.

Using those guidelines, the transfer rate can be defined as *all students entering the community college in a given year who have no prior college experience and who complete at least twelve college-credit units, divided into the number of that group who take one or more classes at the university within four years.*

Transfer Assembly Methodology

The staff of the Center for the Study of Community Colleges began the project by inviting samples of the nation's community colleges to participate in the Transfer Assembly. Initially, the 240 colleges with at least 25 percent minority enrollment made up the invitation list because the Ford Foundation was particularly interested in the progress of minority students. The first round of requests in 1989 found 48 of the invited institutions able to provide the data on the students who had entered their college in 1984 with no prior college experience and who had begun course work at a university by 1989. In the following year, the same 240 were again asked to provide data, this time on their 1985 entrants; 114 colleges participated. In 1991, the sample of colleges invited was expanded and 155 colleges participated.

In 1992, the Transfer Assembly began seeking the data from the state agencies as well as from the colleges. The reason for this shift was that individual community colleges can provide data on the number of students who entered in a given year with no prior college experience and on the number of that group who completed at least twelve college-credit units, but they cannot typically provide information on the number of that group who matriculated at a university. The first two data elements can be derived from the community

Exhibit 7.1. Ford Foundation/Center for the Study of Community Colleges
1993 Transfer Rate Data Form

	BLACK	HISPANIC	AMERICAN INDIAN	WHITE	ASIAN/ PAC. ISLAN.	OTHER	TOTAL
Line 1 Number of students entering your college in fall 1987 with no prior college experience.	___	___	___	___	___	___	___
Line 2 Number of the fall 1987 entrants with no prior college experience who completed 12 or more semester credits* by spring 1991	___	___	___	___	___	___	___
Line 3 Number of the fall 1987 entrants with no prior college experience who completed 12 or more semester credits* and who transferred to senior institutions.	___	___	___	___	___	___	___

*Quarter credits must be transformed to semester credits.

Student data were obtained by (circle one):   student surveys   senior institution   state agency   other
If you obtained your student transfer data from senior institutions, please list which institutions gave you the data:

Your Name: _____
College: _____
State: _____
Telephone _____
FAX Number _____

Return completed form to: Center for the Study of Community Colleges, 1749 Mandeville Lane, Los Angeles, CA 90049 college's own student information system, whereas the data on students who took classes at a university must be obtained from the receiving institutions. (See Transfer Rate Data Form, Exhibit 7.1).

Soliciting the requisite information from the state higher education agencies proved somewhat more fruitful. A few states have coordinated student information systems and were able to generate community college and university student information from that source; New York, Kentucky, and Colorado are examples of such states. Other states have centralized community college databases that could be matched with centralized public university databases; Illinois and North Carolina are examples of such systems. And in others there is a centralized public university student information system against which matches can be run if the data on entering students who receive twelve units can be obtained from the community colleges; Texas and California exemplify such states, the latter having two central data systems, one for the California State University system and the other for the University of California.

The National Transfer Rate

The transfer rates for each year of the Transfer Assembly are detailed in Table 7.1.

Participants

By soliciting data from the state agencies the number of colleges participating increased considerably in the most recent year. The latest figures display data on student transfer from the institutions with more than 40 percent of the enrollment in the nation's public community colleges. In Fall 1987, these colleges served as the point of first entry to higher education for 507,757 students; 237,965 of these students received at least 12 credits at the college they entered; and by 1991, 53,836 of the latter had transferred to a baccalaureate degree-granting institution.

Included in the 366 colleges that provided data on their 1987 entrants were all or most of the public community colleges in California, Colorado, Illinois, Indiana, Kentucky, Louisiana, Massachusetts, Minnesota, New York,

Table 7.1. Transfer Rates, 1984–1987

Number of Participating Colleges	Year Students Entered	Number of Entrants	Percentage Receiving 12+ Credits Within Four Years	Percentage Transferring Within Four Years
48	1984	77,903	50.5	23.7
114	1985	191,748	46.7	23.6
155	1986	267,150	46.7	23.4
366	1987	507,757	46.9	22.6

North Carolina, Rhode Island, Washington, West Virginia, and Wisconsin, plus a few colleges from 16 other states. Following is the number of participating colleges in each state: Alabama (3); California (61); Colorado (17); Florida (1); Georgia (2); Illinois (50); Indiana (14); Kansas (2); Kentucky (14); Louisiana (4); Maryland (3); Massachusetts (15); Michigan (1); Missouri (1); Minnesota (18); Mississippi (1); New Jersey (1); New Mexico (1); New York (24); North Carolina (52); Ohio (1); Oklahoma (2); Oregon (1); Pennsylvania (2); Rhode Island (1); South Carolina (1); Texas (21); Washington (27); West Virginia (11); and Wisconsin (13).

There are 968 public community colleges in the United States; an extrapolation from our sample shows that about 1.25 million students entered those colleges in the fall of 1987. Of those, 573,000 completed twelve or more units and just under 130,000 transferred within four years.

Discussion

Is the definition valid? It fits well with other indicators of college contributions to student progress, most of which establish a specific cohort and then track its movement through the institutions and into succeeding endeavors. The definition's chief limitation is that, by omitting the students who take longer than four years to transfer, it yields an undercount. Many students take more time from initial entry to transfer; several studies have identified transfers who show up in universities ten years and more after community college matriculation. Holding the books open for two or three years longer would add a few percentage points to the transfer rate, especially in higher education systems that expect transferring students to have earned a minimum number of credits (Garcia, 1992).

A second limitation is that it is not feasible to trace students who transfer to universities in other states. The state-level, public system databases do not include out-of-state transfers, a group that certainly accounts for a few additional students.

The students transferring to in-state, independent universities represent a third limitation that adds to the undercount. In most states the independent sector is not included in the accessible databases but in some, such as New York, it is a major receiver of community college transfers.

Taken together, these limitations point to the difficulty of obtaining uniform data across institutional systems. Other types of criticisms have been raised, in some cases by commentators who have proposed definitional modifications that, if utilized, would increase the colleges' transfer rate by depressing the denominator. Their comments have centered on two points: the curriculum that students follow, and student intentions or aspirations.

The curriculum issue usually raised is that the students who take occupational classes should not be included in the denominator. The Assembly leaves them in because many occupational classes (62 percent in California) are in fact transferable to a state university (Cohen and Ignash, 1993). Furthermore, the Center staff could not quite figure out how to categorize the students whose transcripts show an indistinct path; two courses per term, for example, one in English, the other in Keyboarding; one in History, the other in Small-Business Management. Are such students properly classified as university or workforce-bound?

Students' intentions undoubtedly influence their actions, but for several reasons they are unusable in a study of this type. First, not all colleges ask about them and the Transfer Assembly depends on data collected uniformly across the nation. Second, the way that the question is phrased among the colleges that do ask it severely biases the responses. The open-end question, "What is the highest academic degree that you intend to obtain?" yields answers quite different from, "What is the most important reason that you are attending this college at this time?" Third, many students switch intentions after one or two college terms. The students who declare occupational intent at first enrollment but who subsequently say they want to transfer deserve consideration; they have been warmed up, as it were, and the college deserves credit for their progress. In both examples, curriculum paths and declared intentions, the students' eventual behavior speaks for itself.

Although the Transfer Assembly was not designed to answer it, an intriguing question is, What happens to the students who enter but do not complete four courses in four years? This early-attrition phenomenon has long been noted. For example, the California Statewide Longitudinal Study (Hunter and Sheldon, 1980) found numerous students enrolling but never attending classes or attending classes but dropping them before the end of the first term. After interviewing a number of these early leavers the researchers concluded that "most of the reasons given for class drops do not involve issues over which the college has a great deal of control or responsibility" (p. 31). The Transfer Assembly chose not to consider these marginal enrollees in the transfer-rate calculation because the college staff may never have even seen them. Nor did it consider the students who took a summer class on their way to freshman matriculation at a university. In neither case should the community college be held accountable for the students' eventual entry, or lack of entry, in a baccalaureate-granting institution.

The year-to-year consistency in both the percentage of entering students who completed 12 or more credits within four years and the percentage who transferred is notable, especially because the sample of colleges increased each year. Still, the national transfer rate of 22.6 percent masks many differences between institutions and between states. In California, for example, the overall transfer rate for the 61 community colleges that participated in the study was 22 percent, but the range was from 3 to 42 percent. Similarly, even though the transfer rate in most of the states with comprehensive community college systems clustered around the 22.6 percent national mark, the individual states ranged from 11 to 40 percent.

Some of the reasons for this wide between-state disparity are obviously related to state-system structures. In states where the two-year institutions are organized as branch campuses of the state university, the transfer rates are high. In states where the colleges are organized as technical institutes that emphasize trade and industry programs, the transfer rates are low. However, deviations from the comprehensive-college norm appear also in states where policies related to enrollment have been effected in recent years. State-mandated limitations on college growth, for example, eventually elevate the transfer rate because the colleges tend to react to enrollment caps by cutting the programs that attract adult, part-time students; that is, those least likely to transfer.

The within-state differences in transfer rates are even greater than the between-state differences. In states that have both comprehensive and technical colleges, the differences are predictable. But where the colleges all ostensibly provide the same types of programs, the reasons for the disparities must be traced to local conditions. Some of these conditions, such as community demographics and the college's proximity to a university campus, are immutable. Others, such as local employment or economic conditions, are beyond college control. When these powerful forces are factored out, the influence of staff-generated practices pales. However, those efforts deserve analysis because they do have an effect, often on specifically targeted student groups.

Conclusion

The Transfer Assembly set out to provide an answer to the question, What is the community colleges' contribution to their students' progress toward the baccalaureate? The project found that 22.6 percent of the students who began their postsecondary studies in a community college and completed at least four courses there enrolled in a public in-state university within four years. This affords a consistent measure demonstrating that the colleges are serving effectively as the point of entry toward a baccalaureate for a sizable percentage of their entrants, many of whom would not otherwise have been able to matriculate in a freshman class.

What can be done with the data? For the analyst seeking evidence of the American community colleges' role, a set of data collected uniformly across the states is indispensable. For the state-level commentator or system coordinator, the data provide a benchmark for comparing the state's transfer rate with indicators of college accomplishment in other areas: workforce development, literacy training, career upgrading.

The transfer rate indicator is also useful for individual colleges seeking to estimate the effects of various interventions. As a college views its own transfer rate from year to year, the staff can consider what happens when more resources are devoted to articulation agreements, financial aid, transfer centers, orientation programs, counseling interventions, and curriculum modifications. Subcategories can be developed by the institutional researcher who wants to know what happens to the transfer rate when it is modified by student demographics or aspirations, particular courses taken, or participation in special activities (see, for example, Armstrong and Takahata, 1993). Whether or not the administration or the governing board wants to emphasize the transfer function, at least they have a database from which the effects of institutional augmentations or detractions can be viewed. In general, the Transfer Assembly is providing a continuing, databased view from which the community colleges' actual contributions to student progress toward the baccalaureate are emerging.

References

Armstrong, W. B., and Takahata, G. "Building Indicators of Transfer Effectiveness for the San Diego Community College District: A Local Application of the Transfer Assembly Approach." Paper presented at the annual national convention of the American Association of Community Colleges, Portland, Oregon, April 28–May 1, 1993.

Astin. A. W. *What Matters in College?* San Francisco: Jossey-Bass, 1993.

Cohen, A. M. "Building Indicators of Community College Outcomes." Paper presented to the Society of College and University Planners, Seattle, Wash., July 1991. (ED 338 298)

Cohen, A. M., and Ignash, J. M. "The Scope and Transferability of Occupational Courses in the Two-Year College." *Community College Review,* Winter 1993, 21(3), 68–76.

Garcia, P. "Operationalizing the Transfer Function." Paper presented at "Leadership 2000," the fourth annual international conference of the League for Innovation in the Community College, Chicago, July 1992. (ED 344 652)

Hunter, R., and Sheldon, M. S. *Statewide Longitudinal Study. Report on Academic Year 1978–1979. Part I, Fall Results.* Woodland Hills, Calif.: Los Angeles Pierce College, 1980. (ED 180 530)

Orfield, G., and Paul, F. G. "State Higher Education Systems and College Completion." Final Report to the Ford Foundation, Nov. 1992. (ED 354 041)

ARTHUR M. COHEN is director of the ERIC Clearinghouse for Community Colleges and professor of higher education at the University of California, Los Angeles.

Is there a relationship between the curriculum and student transfer rates? Does offering more liberal arts courses or more advanced-level courses promote higher student transfer rates?

Examining the Relationship Between the Liberal Arts, Course Levels, and Transfer Rates

William B. Armstrong, Melissa Mellissinos

The transfer function has historically been perhaps the most important component of the community college mission. Often cited as the raison d'être of the first generation of community colleges, the transfer function has traditionally been characterized by curricular patterns emulating the first two years of baccalaureate education at universities. Curricular patterns and content emphasized the liberal arts both in breadth and content. Courses for university transfer were to be parallel in content, teaching, and texts to be accepted by the universities. The influence of the universities on the first generation of community colleges (in some cases they actually served as accrediting bodies) helped to shape a liberal arts emphasis in two-year colleges. The liberal arts emphasis was noted in studies conducted during the first decades of the two-year colleges. Koos (1925) found the liberal arts and transfer orientation courses to be the most prominent course offerings in the community colleges. In 1930, Eells surveyed 279 junior colleges and found few differences between the curricula presented in junior colleges and in private denominational and independent institutions (Eells, 1931). During this time the universities began to accept this "collegiate function" and admitted transferring students to junior and senior level standing, accepting as equivalent the two years of lower-division coursework completed at the community college. However, in succeeding generations of the two-year college, this university preparation function began to diminish in relative importance because of the rapid expansion of the scope and mission of the "comprehensive" community college.

Expansion of Mission and Decline in the Collegiate Function

The growth in areas such as community studies, career and developmental education, and general interest courses reflected both the changing characteristics of students coming to the colleges and changes in the societal mores. The colleges started to offer courses designed to meet a variety of interests, needs, and attitudes, from liberal arts to community fairs. At the same time, the watchword for the community colleges became access: access for all people of any age, for any purpose (Cohen and Brawer, 1982). Thus the consumerism that became the hallmark of high school education earlier in this century became the hallmark of community colleges in the late 1960s and 1970s. This consumerism was characterized by students as client-consumers dictating the terms under which they would study, and what they expected to gain from their efforts. This feature was demanded by students, and encouraged by policymakers through funding mechanisms that encouraged rapid growth, wide latitude in course approval policies, and general decline in inter-institutional articulation policies (Kintzer, 1981). This resulted in an educational supermarket, where customer preferences, at least in the 1970s, were primarily instrumental and utilitarian.

Rediscovering the Collegiate Function

In the mid 1980s the policy pendulum began to swing back in the direction of collegiate function, transfer, and career education. Policymakers, educators, and legislators began to demand a return to the basics of education that emphasized traditional academic values. In California, for example, the role of community colleges in the State Master Plan for Higher Education as transfer institutions was reaffirmed and mandated by legislative statute (California State Legislature, 1987). Thus were the colleges caught in a paradox: For the last decade or so, they had been rewarded for encouraging attendance and offering a diversity of courses ranging from personal growth to collegiate honors that responded to student and legislative demands for relevancy. However, the legislative re-emphasis on the collegiate and transfer function, with its emphasis on student success as defined by persistence, course sequencing, and transfer rates, marked a significant change in how the colleges were to be judged and funded by legislators. Legislative demands for accountability and indicators of effectiveness reflected the general belief that this reaffirmation of the collegiate mission of the two-year college would increase the transfer of students to senior institutions.

Factors Affecting Transfer

Knoell (1982) and Lombardi (1979) identified and discussed several factors that explain the growth or decline of the transfer rate. Factors cited include the pressure of four-year institutions to improve access and outcomes for histori-cally underrepresented students, the declining economic value of a college degree, and an attitude on the part of the public that higher education has lit-tle value for many people now attending college. Related to these are changes in student demographics and declines in academic preparation, the rise in stu-dent consumerism in the colleges, the decline of rigid course-taking patterns, the tracking of liberal arts and vocational students, and the "all things to all people" approach of the community colleges. Other factors thought to affect transfer include the projection of declining enrollments leading to unused space in four-year institutions, the addition of remedial programs in the uni-versities, and the responsiveness of these institutions to increased student inter-est in preparation for employment after graduation.

Researchers have also sought to relate student transfer to other variables. Astin (1982) suggested that transfer and bachelor's degree completion were related to students' aspiration to transfer, academic preparation, commitment to college, age, hours worked per week, and involvement with the institution (such as student government, working on campus, and participation in stu-dent associations). Banks (1991) hypothesized a relationship between transfer rates and articulation agreements, tuition, college policies regarding academic progress, full-time equivalent (FTE) expenditures per student, percentage of full-time faculty, institutional governance, local employment rates, income, institutional climate, and convenient course scheduling of liberal arts courses. The strength of the liberal arts curriculum has also been cited as an influence on transfer activities (American Council on Education, 1991; Greenfield, 1988; Watkins, 1989), but empirically establishing this relationship has been prob-lematic.

Course Level

The courses offered at remedial or advanced levels have also been noted in rela-tionship to student transfer. The colleges offer developmental coursework and support services to remediate academically disadvantaged students. The occur-rence of students entering college with weak basic skills is not a new phenom-enon. The presence of underprepared students dates back to the nineteenth century. Institutional records and various student and faculty publications con-tain evidence that American colleges and universities admitted students far below college-level standards. Faculty and administrators complained about the same academic deficiencies that they complain about today. Underprepared stu-dents lacked spelling, writing, arithmetic, and study skills. In addition, admis-sion and remediation of these underprepared students was as controversial as it is today (Brier, 1984).

The question of credibility arises. McGrath and Spear (1991) point out that the transfer function originally served to establish the academic legitimacy of the community college. Some educators believe that community colleges serving a large underprepared student population may not transfer students successfully. Remediation is resource-intensive and costly. Developmental students require more individualized instruction and support services than well-prepared students. The assumption is that students lack the skills, not the ability, to perform at college level. Committing resources to developmental education could lead to the de-emphasis of advanced coursework. But this is debatable. Can a community college that serves a developmental student population effectively remediate students so that they can succeed in college-level courses? Remediating underprepared students means helping them develop basic skills in reading, writing, and computation so that they can become functionally literate. One way to remediate students is to place them into English and mathematics classes until they develop skills necessary for college-level courses (or until they become functionally literate). This is called *tracking*. Another method, called *mainstreaming,* is to teach basic skills concurrently with other college-level material. Tracking versus mainstreaming is a controversial issue and community colleges are experimenting with programs to determine which method more effectively increases student success. English and mathematics, which develop skills fundamental to other disciplines, make up nearly the entire remedial curriculum. Entering students who are academically underprepared for college-level work are usually tracked into English and mathematics, where they must demonstrate a functional level of proficiency before they can enroll in other subjects. Ideally the student will develop basic skills and progress into college-level courses that carry degree or transfer credit. Some educators believe that remedial classes are temporary holding tanks for underprepared students who cannot succeed in college-level courses. They expect students to eventually drop out or "cool out" rather than persist. But students can benefit from remediation and proceed to transfer or accomplish another educational goal.

The Sophomore Year

While educating underprepared students in basic skills, community colleges also specialize in freshman and sophomore curriculum for students who plan to transfer. Students planning to transfer may or may not be eligible for admission to a senior institution upon entering the community college. But they are promised the opportunity to complete lower-division coursework at the community college. Can a student complete the freshman and sophomore years at a community college and transfer to a four-year college or university? Specifically, are course levels and transfer related?

This chapter examines the transfer issue from a curricular perspective. Specifically, what relation, if any, exists between the proportion of liberal arts course offerings and transfer rates? Testing these relationships is empirically difficult. Although there are studies documenting the changes in liberal arts courses and the rise in vocational courses in the colleges, it has been more difficult to establish the relationship between these changes in the curriculum and changes in transfer rates and activities. To help establish relationships between curriculum and student behavior, two databases of research conducted by the Center for the Study of Community Colleges were merged. Data on liberal arts offerings in community colleges from around the nation were merged with transfer rate information for these same colleges obtained from their participation in the 1992 Transfer Assembly. Comparison of the two databases indicated that fifty-two colleges participated in both studies and each had useful data for both the liberal arts and transfer rates. Data from these colleges were then used to test the hypothesis of a relation between community college transfer rates and the proportion of liberal arts course offerings.

Method and Analysis

To test the relation between the proportion of liberal arts courses and transfer rates, two analyses were conducted. The first involved a recategorization of both the transfer and liberal arts ratios into high and low categories. Sample means for both ratios were derived. Colleges with transfer rates below the mean of 25 percent were placed in the low category and colleges with transfer rates at or above the mean were placed in the high category. Similarly, colleges with liberal arts ratios at or above the mean of 54 percent were placed in the high category, and those with ratios below 54 percent were placed in the low category. These categories were cross-tabulated, with results as shown in Figure 8.1.

Among those community colleges with transfer rates below the sample mean (less than 25 percent), approximately 69 percent were also below the mean for the proportion of liberal arts offerings in the college and approximately 31.4 percent were above the sample mean of 53 percent. Among those colleges with a transfer rate classified as high, approximately 38 percent were low in liberal arts and approximately 63 percent were high in liberal arts offerings. The chi-square test of independence suggests a statistically significant relation between the two categories; analysis of the chi-square residuals indicates that colleges with below-average liberal arts ratios also have disproportionately low transfer rates, while colleges above the mean liberal arts ratio tend to have higher transfer rates. To further test the direction of these differences, the liberal arts and transfer ratios were further subdivided into four categories (Very High, High, Low, Very Low). These were then cross-tabulated and the results shown in Figure 8.2. Although there appears to be a moderate relation between these two variables when examined in this way, the chi-square statistic was not significant at the .05 level.

As is shown in Figure 8.1, colleges with Very High and High proportions of liberal arts offerings are positively associated with higher transfer rates.

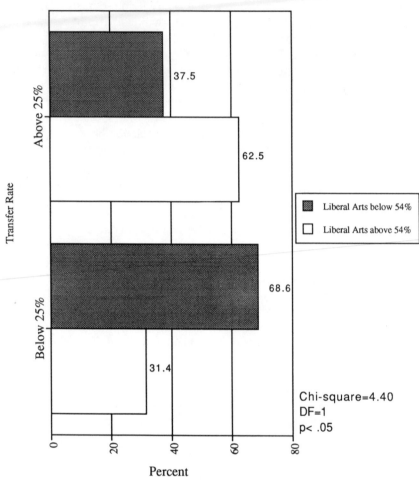

Figure 8.1 Comparison of High/Low Transfer Rates
and High/Low Proportion of Liberal Arts

Among colleges with a Very Low proportion of liberal arts offerings, none were classified as Very High with respect to transfer. Although a relationship between varying proportions of liberal arts and varying levels of transfer is suggested by Figure 8.2, the results are not conclusive.

Are the Liberal Arts Related to Transfer Rates?

A second analysis was conducted to determine if variance in observed transfer rates could be explained by variance in the percent of liberal arts offerings. A

Figure 8.2 Comparison of Transfer Rates with Proportion of Liberal Arts Offerings

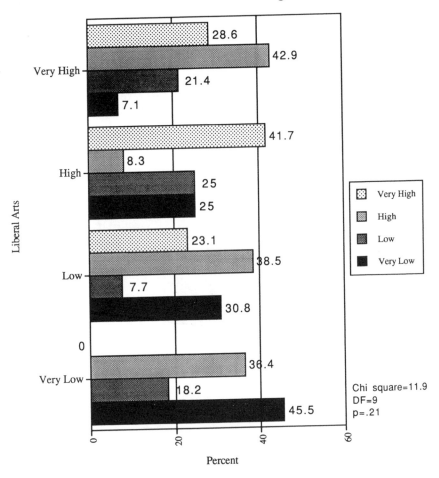

correlational analysis was conducted to test this hypothesis using the college transfer rate as the dependent variable and proportion of liberal arts courses, recoded for size (Size: Small, Size: Medium, and Size: Large) and by level (remedial, standard, and advanced) as dummy variables. These data were analyzed using the SPSS Correlation procedure and a one-tail test of significance was performed. The results of this analysis are presented in Table 8.1.

Correlation Analysis

As suggested by the cross-tabulations presented earlier, there is a significant positive correlation ($p < .05$) between transfer rate and proportion of liberal

Table 8.1. Correlation Analysis

	Transfer Rate	% Liberal Arts	% Remedial	% Standard	% Advanced	Size			% Nonwhite
						Small	Medium	Large	
Transfer Rate	1.000	.345*	-.159	.056	.041	-.088	.108	-.058	-.191
% Liberal Arts	.345*	1.000	-.139	.160	-.095	-.250	-.173	.305	.115
% Remedial	-.159	-.139	1.000	-.541	-.038	.100	.174	-.223	.050
% Standard	.056	.160	-.541	1.000	-.820	.036	-.147	.124	.076
% Advanced	.041	-.095	-.038	-.820	1.000	-.111	.057	.005	-.124
Size									
Small	-.088	-.250	.100	.036	-.111	1.000	-.231	-.319*	-.172
Medium	.108	-.173	.174	-.147	.057	-.231	1.000	-.848**	-.270
Large	-.058	.305	-.223	.124	.005	-.319*	-.848**	1.000	.356*
% Nonwhite	-.191	.115	.050	.076	-.124	-.172	-.270	.356	1.000

* Significant at .05 (one-tail).

** Significant at .01 (one-tail).

arts courses. Large colleges were positively related with percent of liberal arts sections, whereas small and medium-sized colleges were negatively correlated. Percent nonwhite was found to be negatively related to transfer rate. Interestingly, college size is either not related or has a slight negative relationship to transfer rates.

The results of the correlation analysis indicate that although several variables are positively related to transfer rate, only the percent of liberal arts variable is related at the .05 level. Although the percent of liberal arts course offerings at the colleges in the sample appears to be positively related to transfer rates, there are probably several other factors not specified that would probably explain greater variance in transfer than merely the proportion of liberal arts offerings alone.

Various statistical methods were also used to understand the relationship between remedial curriculum and transfer. No clear relationship between the percent of remedial course offerings in the liberal arts and transfer was found. The percentage of remedial course offerings is not correlated to transfer rate and holds no predictive value. A chi-square test revealed that community colleges with large percentages of remedial course offerings did not have lower transfer rates. However, the findings indicate that community colleges with more than half the remedial curriculum in English tend to have lower transfer rates than schools that offer more remedial math.

Remedial courses account for about 11 percent and advanced ("sophomore level") course offerings for about 21 percent of the liberal arts curriculum in community colleges. Nearly all the remedial courses are in English or math. Most of the advanced classes are in humanities (22 percent), followed by English (19 percent), science (18 percent), fine and performing arts (17 percent), mathematics/computer science (17 percent), and social science (7 percent).

Advanced liberal arts curriculum also appeared unrelated to transfer rate. Community colleges offering a greater percentage of advanced liberal arts course offerings do not have higher transfer rates, nor do schools with high concentrations of advanced courses in specific disciplines. Hybrid disciplines were created by combining related disciplines, but provided no additional insight into the relationship between curriculum and transfer.

The distribution of remedial, standard, and advanced course offerings varies significantly. Only one school in the sample of 52 that participated in the curriculum and transfer studies offered more than 40 percent of its curriculum at the remedial level, whereas seven schools offered more than 40 percent at the advanced level. The percent of remedial course offerings is not correlated to the percent of advanced course offerings, and they are both negatively correlated to college size.

Larger schools show less differentiation in the course levels. They offer more standard (freshman or "college-level") courses and less remedial and advanced courses. But more differentiated schools do not differ in transfer rates from the more homogeneous schools that offer primarily college-level courses. Furthermore, schools with skewed advanced course offerings (compared to remedial) do not differ in transfer rates.

English as a Second Language (ESL)

Some educators view ESL as remedial English while others believe that it is a foreign language. In the above analyses, ESL was handled as a foreign language and the ESL courses fell into the standard and advanced categories based on the coding criteria. Because many ESL students are tracked rather than main-streamed, analyses were conducted to determine whether reclassifying ESL as remedial affected the above conclusions.

Thirty-seven percent of ESL classes are offered at the advanced level and the remainder are standard (63 percent). When ESL is classified with remedial curriculum, the percent of remedial course offerings in the liberal arts increases somewhat significantly to 17 percent and the percent of advanced course offerings decreases to 19 percent. The percent of nonwhite students is negatively correlated 31 percent with transfer rate. And although nonwhite schools offer more ESL, regrouping ESL with remedial curriculum does not significantly alter the relationships between remedial and advanced course offerings and transfer.

Conclusion

These findings suggest that precollegiate, freshman, and sophomore stratifications in the curriculum structure are unrelated to transfer. Schools with more remedial curriculum track underprepared students; this requires additional time until the student can become transfer eligible. Remedial education is more resource intensive and provides more opportunity for underprepared students to drop out, but there is no conclusive evidence that emphasized remedial education is inhibiting transfer. On the other hand, schools offering minimal remedial curriculum may be mainstreaming underprepared students into col-lege-level courses, but this also appears to have no impact on transfer.

The prominence of advanced courses varies widely among community colleges. Apparently, a student has more opportunity to complete lower-division baccalaureate coursework and transfer successfully when adequate advanced course offerings are available. Yet this is not reflected in transfer rates. Because transfer rates include students who have completed a minimum of 12 units at the community college before transferring, it is possible that students who can-not take sophomore classes at the community college may transfer early. Also, sophomore-level classes may be only transferable if they are specified in an articulation agreement between the two-year college and the four-year college or university selected by the student.

Although the findings here are tentative, they do lend support to those who have argued that transfer rates are related to variance in liberal arts offerings. However, these findings should be interpreted with caution. It may be the case that differences in liberal arts ratios at certain colleges are related to variances in transfer rates, but other research cited earlier suggests that there are several other factors that help to explain variance in transfer rates among colleges. However, the relationship presented here appears to hold promise and should provide some impetus to examination in more detail. The curriculum data might become part of a model seeking to explain variance in transfer using institutional, organizational, and contextual variables. However they are used, these findings may be useful to those interested in better understanding this often hypothesized association and offer one of the first empirical glimpses of this relationship.

References

American Council on Education. *Setting the National Agenda: Academic Achievement and Transfer.* Washington, D.C.: National Center for Academic Achievement and Transfer, 1991.

Astin, A. W. *Minorities in American Higher Education.* San Francisco: Jossey-Bass, 1982.

Banks, D. L. "Environmental and Organizational Factors Influencing the Community College Transfer Function." Unpublished doctoral dissertation, Graduate School of Education, University of California, Los Angeles, 1991.

Brier, E. "Bridging the Academic Preparation Gap: An Historical View." *Journal of Developmental Education,* 1984, 8 (1), 2–5.

California State Legislature. *"Legislative Council's Digest of the California Community College Reform Act."* Assembly Bill No. 1725. Sacramento: California State Publications, 1987.

Cohen, A. M., and Brawer, F. B. *The American Community College.* San Francisco: Jossey-Bass, 1982.

Eells, W. C. *The Junior College.* Boston: Houghton Mifflin, 1931.

Greenfield, R. K. "Continuation of Community College Vigor: Strengthening the Liberal Arts, General Education, and Transfer Education." In J. S. Eaton (ed.), *Colleges of Choice: The Enabling Impact of the Community College.* New York: Macmillan, 1988.

Kintzer, F. C., (ed.). *Improving Articulation and Transfer Relationships.* New Directions for Community Colleges, no. 39. San Francisco: Jossey-Bass, 1982.

Knoell, D. M. "The Transfer Function—One of Many." In F. C. Kintzer (ed.), *Improving Articulation and Transfer Relationships.* New Directions for Community Colleges, no 39. San Francisco: Jossey-Bass, 1982.

Koos, L. V. *The Junior College Movement.* Boston: Ginn Publishing, 1925.

Lombardi, J. *The Decline of Transfer Education."* Topical Paper No. 70. Los Angeles: ERIC Clearinghouse for Junior Colleges. (ED 179 273)

McGrath, D., and Spear, M. B. *The Academic Crisis of the Community College.* Albany: State University of New York Press, 1991.

Watkins, B. T. "Community Colleges Urged to Bolster Liberal Arts to Help Students Transfer to Four-Year Institutions." *Chronicle of Higher Education,* 1989, 36 (9), A35, A38.

WILLIAM B. ARMSTRONG is director of institutional research at San Diego Community Col-lege District and a doctoral student in higher education at the University of California, Los Angeles.

MELISSA MELLISSINOS is a research analyst at Los Angeles Trade-Technical College.

*Is the community college curriculum a factor in influencing the
transfer rates of minority-group students?*

Curriculum and Minority Students

Shannon M. Hirose

For many people who would not otherwise be able to attend college, community colleges serve as the first entry point into higher education. In comparison to enrollments in other divisions of higher education, minorities are overrepresented at the community college. According to Richardson and Bender (1987), minorities make up 21.2 percent of the community college population, a figure that closely parallels their percentage of the U.S. population. Figures from *Minorities in Higher Education* (American Council on Education, 1990) show the percentage of nonwhite students in two-year institutions in 1988 to be 22 percent. Noting that a large population of community college students is made up of ethnic minority groups, how are community colleges serving this population of students?

There are those who believe that minorities and disadvantaged students usually attend schools that have a large concentration of vocational course offerings, thus tracking these students into a vocational route and leading them away from pursuing bachelor's degrees (Brint and Karabel, 1989; Pincus and Archer, 1989; Richardson and Bender, 1985; Pincus, 1980). Richardson and Bender (1985) would argue that more poor people, immigrants, and minorities live in urban settings than in suburban settings and that community colleges in urban settings tend to place more focus on vocational than on academic programs. Therefore, they conclude that disadvantaged and minority students are exposed to and tracked into vocational rather than academic education. Richardson and Bender (1985) also note that some writers (Astin, 1993; Breneman and Nelson, 1981) conclude that "a narrowing of the curriculum combined with low completion rates [of community colleges] . . . do not really serve the interests of students coming directly from high school to pursue careers requiring the baccalaureate degree" (p. 10). In other words, these writers feel that community colleges are not providing students with education that is conducive to or that leads to transfer.

Pincus (1980) observes that there is a higher proportion of working class and nonwhites concentrated in vocational rather than transfer programs in community colleges. "This stratification within . . . community colleges tends to reproduce the class and racial inequalities existing in the larger society" (Pincus, 1980, p. 334). Although without direct evidence to support their claim, Lee and Frank (1990) also believe that for students who are not prepared for or motivated in the academic direction, there is less of an emphasis on academic programs and more on vocational programs in these community colleges.

With the concern for vocational education tracking students away from the baccalaureate degree there has also been some concern about its effect on transfer. Grubb (1991) attributes declining transfer rates to a weakening in academic programs and the offering of only a few courses taught beyond the introductory level at community colleges. Lee and Frank (1990) suggest that an emphasis on vocational education may lead to lower transfer rates of students with poor academic backgrounds. If these contentions are valid, the curriculum and transfer rates at colleges with high proportions of minorities should reflect the differences. What does the curriculum at schools with a large percentage of nonwhites look like? Do schools with large concentrations of ethnic minority students offer fewer liberal arts classes? Do they offer more remedial courses? Do community colleges with large numbers of minority students have lower transfer rates than those with smaller numbers of minority students?

Findings

Fifty-two community colleges across the United States participated in both the Center for the Study of Community College (CSCC) 1991 Curriculum Project and 1992 Transfer Assembly Project. By combining information from the databases of these two projects with U.S. Department of Education data on student enrollments (*Almanac of Higher Education,* 1991), observations about the relationship between the percentage of nonwhite students and curriculum and transfer were made.

For this sample of the fifty-two community colleges that overlapped both studies, the mean percentage of nonwhite (black, Hispanic, American Indian, Asian) enrollment is 48.7 percent. This number is higher than the national average of two-year colleges, due to the sampling techniques employed by the Transfer Assembly project, which in earlier years recruited only schools with more than 20 percent ethnic minority composition. The mean transfer rate for these fifty-two colleges is 24.6 percent, slightly higher than the total sample of the 1992 Transfer Assembly (23.4 percent). The average percentage of liberal arts course offerings at these fifty-two colleges is 57.5 percent, about one percentage point higher than the total sample average. Table 9.1 shows a break-

Table 9.1. Percentage of Nonwhite Students, Percentage of Liberal
Arts Offerings, and Transfer Rates by College

College Code	Percentage Nonwhite	Percentage Liberal Arts	Transfer Rate
IL03	2.0	48.4	32.6
WY02	4.0	44.0	34.0
WY01	7.4	49.5	50.6
OH01	9.0	51.0	25.0
IL06	10.0	44.0	21.0
PA02	12.2	66.0	19.1
KY01	14.0	65.4	29.2
TX15	14.8	71.8	53.3
TX07	16.0	52.0	28.0
MS01	19.1	54.0	36.3
TX18	21.0	30.0	5.0
TX12	23.0	61.0	39.0
KS03	24.0	46.0	24.0
CA28	24.0	68.0	23.0
NM02	24.2	53.7	16.9
TX16	25.3	53.9	76.3
IL10	28.3	39.9	20.8
CA15	33.0	47.0	5.0
SC02	36.0	26.5	6.5
CA25	36.0	63.0	20.0
TX13	38.3	57.0	33.2
NC07	39.0	42.0	23.0
NC02	42.7	39.2	2.0
CA04	43.6	56.5	19.3
IL05	44.2	65.2	27.9
CA14	45.0	58.0	16.0
NC09	47.9	20.1	13.0
CA20	48.3	53.6	22.9
PA03	49.0	75.0	48.0
CA12	49.0	63.0	21.0
CA16	50.0	56.0	21.0
AR02	50.0	38.0	21.0
CA30	52.0	54.0	19.0
TX05	52.0	58.0	25.0
IL01	54.5	68.8	24.6
CA03	56.2	62.2	14.1
TX02	57.0	49.4	21.4
CA31	59.8	47.9	18.2
CA13	64.9	50.7	20.6
CA06	65.0	46.4	21.1
KS01	65.4	67.1	40.0
CA11	65.9	58.9	17.5
FL04	69.0	75.0	26.0
NJ01	71.5	76.7	7.1
IL07	73.7	67.8	19.4
NJ03	74.0	84.0	18.0

Table 9.1. (*continued*)

College Code	Percentage Nonwhite	Percentage Liberal Arts	Transfer Rate
CA33	80.5	35.3	18.7
CA27	87.0	62.0	20.0
NY07	90.7	70.6	20.1
GA02	91.2	78.5	26.9
TX06	N/A	58.4	32.1
CA22	N/A	51.0	18.0
	$\bar{x} = 48.7$	$\bar{x} = 57.5$	$\bar{x} = 24.6$

down of percentage of nonwhite students, transfer rate, and percentage of liberal arts course offerings at each of the fifty-two community colleges. As shown with the line drawn through Table 9.1, thirty-nine colleges have a nonwhite percentage population mean falling above the national average of 22 percent, eleven colleges fall below the average, and for two, the ethnic breakdown was not available.

Nonwhite Students and Curriculum

Is there a relationship between the percentage of nonwhite students at a community college and the type of curriculum offered? If, as many commentators suggest, the colleges tend not to provide collegiate courses to the ethnic minority students, it would follow that the larger the percentage of nonwhites, the lower the percentage of liberal arts course offerings. Using percentage of nonwhite students as the independent variable and percentage of liberal arts offerings as the dependent variable, a simple correlation was run. The result was a significant relationship ($p \geq .05$) of .32. This means that the larger the population of nonwhite students at a community college the greater the proportion of liberal arts courses offered.

What level of courses are the community colleges offering their students? Are minorities attending schools with more remedial courses and not enough standard and advanced courses? To test the relationships between these variables, correlations were run between the percentage of nonwhite students and the percentage of remedial, standard, and advanced courses of the liberal arts curriculum. (For example, the percentage of remedial liberal arts classes was calculated by dividing the total number of liberal arts sections into the number of remedial liberal arts sections.) These correlations reflected no significant relationships between the ethnic composition of a school and the percentage of remedial, standard, and advanced courses in the liberal arts curriculum. This would seem to indicate that there are no significant differences in the level of course offerings in schools with relation to the ethnic composition.

In light of the correlations that were run, it does not seem that the community college curriculum is tracking ethnic minority students into vocational education. A strongly positive correlation was found between the percentage of nonwhite students and the percentage of liberal arts courses. Overall, therefore, ethnic minorities are not necessarily attending schools which emphasize vocational programs. For example, at Atlanta Metropolitan in Georgia, 91 percent of the student population is nonwhite, and 79 percent of the curriculum is devoted to liberal arts. At Borough of Manhattan Community College in New York, a similar pattern emerges with nonwhite students comprising 91 percent of the population and liberal arts constituting 71 percent of the curriculum. In comparison, colleges that have smaller percentages of nonwhites, such as Williamsburg Technical College in South Carolina (36 percent nonwhite) and Triton College in Illinois (28 percent nonwhite), have percentages of liberal arts curriculums that fall below the 57.5 percent mean.

However, noting that English as a Second Language (ESL) was coded under liberal arts and that a community college with a large nonwhite population may offer more ESL classes than a college with a smaller nonwhite population, another correlation was run with ESL sections extracted from the percentage of liberal arts course offerings. Although it did not remain significant, the correlation continued to reveal a positive relationship (.19). Therefore, even while controlling for ESL, the contention that colleges with high proportions of minorities tend to offer fewer liberal arts classes is still not supported. Even with ESL taken out of the liberal arts, the percentage of liberal arts courses offered at Atlanta Metropolitan College and Borough of Manhattan Community College remained above the mean—68 percent and 60 percent, respectively. It appears that ethnic minorities do have access to liberal arts curricula and college-level courses. Also, when looking at the correlations between percent nonwhite and the percentage of remedial, standard, and advanced liberal arts courses, there were no significant relationships. This would indicate that minorities are not necessarily attending schools that offer few or no courses beyond the introductory level. The insignificant relationships would seem to imply that colleges with large ethnic minority populations do not offer any more or less liberal arts courses at the remedial, standard, or advanced level than colleges with smaller ethnic minority populations. Overall, data from the 1991 curriculum project show that colleges with a large percentage of nonwhite students do not differ in their course offerings from colleges with lower percentages of nonwhite students.

During the following 1993 Transfer Assembly project, the CSCC calculated transfer rates for the students who entered 366 community colleges in fall, 1987, and transferred to a public, in-state university by fall, 1991; 211 community colleges provided these data according to students' ethnicity. Their findings are detailed in Table 9.2.

Table 9.2. Mean Transfer Rates for Students in 211 Colleges

| | Ethnic Groups | | | | |
	Black	Hispanic	Asian	White	Total
All colleges	15.3	16.0	24.7	25.6	23.4
Top quartile	24.9	30.9	34.7	35.6	34.4
Bottom quartile	10.6	9.5	14.6	13.6	12.2

The CSCC found that transfer rates for Hispanic and black students were well below those of Asian and white students. The top performing 53 colleges show transfer rates well above the state averages for all ethnic groups. The 53 bottom performing colleges show transfer rates well below the state averages for all ethnic groups. These results suggest that the various ethnic groups are receiving roughly the same benefit from the transfer programs and practices at high and low performing colleges.

Nonwhite Students and Transfer

It is interesting to note that while the curriculum does not seem to differ between community colleges with larger populations of nonwhites and smaller populations of nonwhites, transfer rates do. Running a correlation with percent nonwhite and transfer rate, a significant negative relationship ($p \geq .05$) of −.31 was found. The larger the percent of nonwhite, the lower the transfer rate. So, although a higher concentration of minority students at community colleges is related to larger amounts of liberal arts course offerings, it is also related to a lower transfer rate.

In addition to the correlation, a cross-tabulation and chi-square were run. The percent of nonwhite students (the independent variable) was divided into two groups—high and low percent of nonwhites—using the mean percentage of nonwhite (48.7 percent) as the cutoff point between the two groups. The dependent variable (transfer rate) was also split into high and low groups using the average transfer rate of the sample (24.6 percent) as the cutoff point. The chi-square reflected a significant relationship at the .04 level. The cross-tabulation revealed that of the colleges with a low percentage of minority students, 56.7 percent had low transfer rates and 43.3 had high transfer rates. Of the colleges with large numbers of minority students, 85.0 percent had low transfer rates and 15.0 had high transfer rates (Figure 9.1). Like the correlation, the cross-tabulation reveals that the larger the percent of nonwhite, the lower the transfer rate. However, it is intriguing to look at the transfer rate groupings. Of the colleges with high transfer rates, 81.3 percent have a small

Figure 9.1 Percentage Nonwhite Students and Transfer Rate

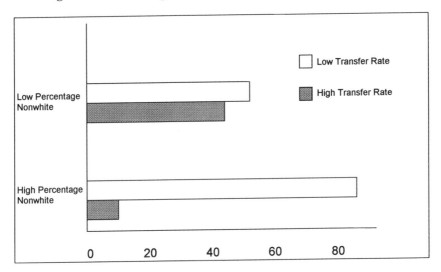

minority enrollment and 18.8 have a large minority enrollment. Of the colleges with low transfer rates, 50 percent are small minority colleges and 50 percent are large minority colleges. This means that while the group of colleges with high transfer rates consists of more colleges with low minority representation, the group of low transfer rate colleges is made up equally of high and low minority college populations. This suggests that when transfer rates of a college are low, there is something about the overall college and not the ethnic composition that brings transfer rates down. Although nonwhite students do not appear to be transferring as much as white students, there seems to be something about low transfer rate colleges that impedes the transfer rates of both white and nonwhite students.

Although low transfer rate colleges affect both white and nonwhite students, why then are ethnic minorities not transferring as often as white students at high transfer rate schools? It does not appear that community colleges impose specific types of curriculum on certain populations. On the contrary, they appear to meet the demand or needs of the population or community they serve. Ethnic minorities do appear to have access to liberal arts curricula and college-level courses. Apparently, curriculum/vocational tracking may not be a cause for lower transfer rates specifically among ethnic minority populations, and that other issues may be a factor in hindering transfer, such as location of a community college, articulation agreements, preparation before entry into college, campus atmosphere, academic counseling, and student goals.

Analyzing the curriculum, community colleges seem to be meeting the needs and demands of their communities. Liberal arts (educational track) and courses at all levels are available to ethnic minority students. Although high transfer rate schools may consist of more white students, low transfer rate schools affect white and minority students equally. It is suggested that other factors that may impede the transfer of minority students be investigated.

References

American Council on Education. *Minorities in Higher Education: Ninth Annual Status Report 1990.* Washington, D.C.: American Council on Education, 1990.

Astin, A. *What Matters in College?* San Francisco: Jossey-Bass, 1993.

Breneman, D., and Nelson, S. *Financing Community Colleges: An Economic Perspective.* Washington D.C.: The Brookings Institution, 1981.

Brint, S., and Karabel, J. *The Diverted Dream: Community Colleges and the Promise of Educational Opportunity in America, 1900–1985.* New York: Oxford University Press, 1989.

Grubb, N. "The Decline of Community College Transfer Rates: Evidence from National Longitudinal Surveys." *Journal of Higher Education,* 1991, 62 (2), 194–222.

Lee, V. E., and Frank, K. A. "Student Characteristics that Facilitate Transfer from Two-Year to Four-Year Colleges." *Sociology of Education,* 1990, 63 (2), 235–254.

Pincus, F. "The False Promises of Community Colleges: Class Conflict and Vocational Education." *Harvard Educational Review,* 1990, 50 (3), 332–361.

Pincus, F., and Archer, E. *Bridges to Opportunity: Are Community Colleges Meeting the Transfer Needs of Minority Students?* New York: Academy for Educational Development and College Entrance Examination Board, 1989.

Richardson, R., and Bender, L. *Students in Urban Settings: Achieving the Baccalaureate Degree.* Washington, D.C.: Association for the Study of Higher Education, 1985.

Richardson, R., and Bender, L. *Fostering Minority Access and Achievement in Higher Education.* San Francisco: Jossey-Bass, 1987.

U.S. Department of Education. *The Almanac of Higher Education.* Chicago: University of Chicago Press, 1991.

SHANNON M. HIROSE is a research assistant at the Center for the Study of Community Colleges and a doctoral student in higher education at the University of California, Los Angeles.

What do the 1990s hold in store for the community college curriculum? What trends are likely to affect the transfer function of the community college?

Conclusion: The Future for Curriculum and Transfer

Arthur M. Cohen

This volume has considered the community college curriculum, student transfer rates, and the relationships between them. The curriculum and the transfer rates have been shown to be stable for the years that the data have been compiled uniformly across the country. Graduation and transfer requirements act to sustain the liberal arts at just over half the college course offerings.

The data reported in this volume demonstrate that the community college collegiate function is intact. Around 130,000 of the 1.25 million students who enter the colleges each year transfer within four years. A few prominent researchers, Orfield and Paul (1992) for example, have noted that if the universities had been open to those 1.25 million students originally, many more would have gone on toward the baccalaureate. But that is a big "if." In most states the option of university attendance is not available to students who have marginal high school records. University tuition is higher than community college tuition; thus university attendance is not open to many low-income people. Furthermore many universities discourage part-time attendance and most community college students attend part-time because of work or other responsibilities. Community colleges are available within commuting distance, allowing students to attend college without having to establish new residential arrangements. For all these reasons, the community college provides opportunity for large numbers of people.

The liberal arts curriculum has also been challenged. For many years community college spokespersons have been emphasizing the institution's occupational role, vocational and technical courses, and contributions to workforce development. When faced with the data showing the liberal arts at 56 percent of the credit courses, those who have labeled the community college as a vocational training center are incredulous. Their preconceptions have been conditioned by several forces: community college leaders who choose to emphasize workforce development because they feel they can derive state support more readily for that function; university-based academicians who contend that community colleges cannot provide a satisfactory lower-division experience; and, not least, academic researchers who are determined to prove that the minority students who enroll in community colleges in greater numbers relative to their total student population than in the universities are being shortchanged. The latter insist that the minorities who go to community colleges enter a cul de sac in their academic progression, that they are tracked into noncollegiate areas, that the community college is a dead-end for them. The data on curriculum and transfer show that those allegations are quite inaccurate.

Transfer Rate Disparities

As numerous studies have shown, the transfer rates are different for different ethnic groups. Whereas the overall transfer rate is 23 percent, it is 25 percent for white and Asian students and 16 percent for Black and Hispanic students. And the transfer rates for individual institutions in the same state are quite disparate; in California they range from 4 to 40 percent and the other states similarly show wide differences. Across the nation, the average gap is 29 percent between the transfer rates of the highest and the lowest college in the same state. In the colleges with the highest transfer rates, the Black and Hispanic students transfer at a rate higher than the overall average for their group. In brief, a college with a high transfer rate has a high transfer rate for everybody. The same pattern holds for colleges at the low end; institutions from which few students transfer depress transfer rates for students of every ethnicity (see Chapter 9, Table 9.2).

The concept of differential transfer rates, with high transfer rate colleges transferring greater numbers of minority as well as majority students, deserves elaboration. The community colleges have expanded opportunity for people to matriculate in higher education. The key to that expansion is lower tuition, acceptance of part-time attendance, forgiveness for past academic sins, and, not least, location. By placing the community colleges within commuting distance of everyone, attendance is made quite easy. The community college and state university in the same town often have curriculum articulation agreements, course equivalency notations, and counselors and faculty working part-time in both institutions, thus effecting a strong link between the two. Universities offering courses at night and welcoming part-time students as well as upper-division state universities such as those in Illinois, Texas, and Washington also enhance transfer.

But the ubiquity of community colleges is not matched by the availability of public universities. A college in a California desert community will attract people who would not otherwise consider higher education. If there is no state university campus within a hundred miles of that community, few students will progress beyond the community college. Isolation is an inhibitor to transfer and it affects students of every ethnicity and socio-economic level.

A second depressant to transfer is the cultivated perception of the community college. If a college has consistently publicized its contract training, low-skill job preparation, and short-term adult studies over a period of years, in effect discouraging transfer-oriented students from attending, it will have a low transfer rate. Similarly, a college with a reputation as a starting place for a baccalaureate will have a high transfer rate. The latter college will have clearly stated articulation agreements with local universities such that prospective students know that they can get the first two years of a specific baccalaureate program at a considerably lower cost than they would have to pay for those two years at the university. In both examples, the messages sent by the colleges are important.

In addition to publicizing what the community colleges do for people beginning postsecondary studies, other uses for the data on curriculum and transfer can be found. Some of the more useful ways of applying the data are to monitor the effects of various programs. If the college has introduced a transfer center or some other major initiative, the data trackers may be able to find out at least inferentially what the effect was. Special programs for special groups can also be monitored. For example, "Did our transfer rate for Hispanic students go up because we have made a special effort to recruit transfer-bound Hispanic students and provide them with specific services?" A set of data collected consistently over the years is essential for answering such questions.

Future of Transfer

Over the next few years the transfer rates should increase because of several conditions that will affect them. For one, the universities that have budgetary problems are cutting back on the number of first-year students they are accepting, thus forcing people beginning higher education to go into the community colleges. This group will include a number of transfer-bound students. The budget limitations have also caused the universities to increase their tuition rates, which again will force many capable students into the community colleges where they can obtain the first two years toward the baccalaureate at a lower cost. This same cost factor is causing additional scrutiny in states that are attempting to hold down the rising costs of higher education in general and are thus putting increasing pressure on the colleges and universities to effect better articulation arrangements.

Budget constraints will also have an effect on transfer-related activities. In contrast to the 1970s when the colleges could set up new programs and find supplemental state funding for them, the 1990s are seeing a limitation on new state monies. As the colleges settle back into their major functional areas of job entry, career upgrading, prebaccalaureate studies, and basic literacy preparation, transfer rates will increase as the peripheral activities such as avocational courses for adults decrease. However, English as a Second Language has been the most rapidly expanding area of the curriculum for several years and shows no sign of abating. Whether or not the courses are offered for transfer credit, they represent a major effort on the part of the colleges that are assisting limited English speakers to enter the workforce and into American society in general.

The increase of the number of 18-year-olds in the American population that began a couple of years ago and will continue until 2003 will also effect higher transfer rates. The 18-year-olds are the traditional transfer students and as greater numbers of them appear, the median age of the community college population will decrease and the transfer rate will increase.

The community college staff members' interest in transfer as a central institutional function has grown as they realize that funding is not available for marginal activities and that full-time staff members who entered the institution with the idea of working in the transfer program remain on staff even as the part-timers and those who are employed for special program activities are dismissed. This has a salutary effect on everything from student recruitment to counseling to curriculum to articulation agreements, all of which are necessary to keep the transfer function in its prominent place. In summation, the 1990s will be a popular decade for those who are committed to the transfer function.

The stability in curriculum will continue as it has for the past fifteen years with the liberal arts and occupational studies dominating. The main casualty will be the avocational and recreational courses offered for college credit. Increasingly, the students who are enrolled in degree or certificate programs will be forced into the noncredit and otherwise self-supporting areas.

The major growth in liberal arts curriculum will continue in English as a Second Language and in business fields in the occupational cluster. Business has a great potential for expansion as more of the courses now offered as noncredit move into degree programs. Many aspects of contract training for industry, for example, can be formed into credit curricula. Testing a set of courses in noncredit programs before integrating them in the regular curriculum is a traditional method of curriculum formation. Growth in the health fields may subside as the proportion of health workers in the U.S. economy slows its expansion. Administration of justice seems to be destined to increase.

These trends happen in all educational sectors. The community colleges are no more or less responsive to curricular shifts in their credit offerings. Along with other types of institutions they have staff members with vested interests whose prior experience and training militate against their rapid adoption of new programs. If enrollments and funding expand, new programs can be added. But because overall expansion in the next few years will be modest, changes will have to occur within existing forms. Thus the traditional staff, organization, and channels serve as an anchor limiting program modification.

References

Orfield, G., and Paul, F. G. "State Higher Education Systems and College Completion. Final Report to the Ford Foundation." New York: Ford Foundation, 1992. (ED 354 041)

ARTHUR M. COHEN *is director of the ERIC Clearinghouse for Community Colleges and professor of higher education at the University of California, Los Angeles.*

INDEX

Advanced courses, 14; percentage of colleges providing, 17
African Americans, 63, 64, 65, 102
Agriculture, 20; number of sections and percentage of courses offered, 22; percentage of total curriculum in, 23
Allen, J. P., 54
Almanac of Higher Education, 94
American Council on Education, 83, 93
Amnesty Act, 54, 58, 59
Archer, E., 93
Armstrong, W. B., 79
Asian Americans, 63, 64
Associate-degree graduation requirements, 43
Association of Community and Junior Colleges, 66
Astin, A. W., 8, 71, 83, 93
Asylees, 53–55
Atlanta Metropolitan, 97
Avocational courses, 21; number of sections and percentage of courses offered, 22; percentage of total curriculum in, 23

Baldwin, A., 55
Banks, D. L., 83
Beauchamp, G. A., 33
Bender, L., 18, 93
Biology, 15
Borough of Manhattan Community College, 97
Brawer, F., 8, 82
Breneman, D., 93
Brier, E., 83
Brint, S., 8, 93
Business and office, 20; number of sections and percentage of courses offered, 22; percentage of total curriculum in, 23

California State University (CSU) system, 24, 25, 28
California Statewide Longitudinal Study, 77

Center for the Study of Community Colleges (CSCC), 13, 32, 36, 43, 45, 49, 50, 64, 65, 71, 73, 74, 85, 94, 97, 98
Cepeda, R., 64
Chavez, M., 63
Chemistry, 15
Chronicle of Higher Education, 55
Clowes, D. A., 31, 32, 33, 37
Cohen, A. M., 8, 82
College size, curriculum patterns and, 17
Collegiate education: defined, 3–5; expansion of mission and decline in function of, 82; rediscovering, 82
Community college: ability to be a collegiate institution, 6–8; as a collegiate institution, 5–6, 7; function of, 5; meaning of collegiate, 8–10; required subjects at, 46
Community College of Philadelphia, 57, 59, 61
Computer sciences: enrollment and average class size in, 16; percentage of colleges offering liberal arts classes in, by institutional size, 19; percentage of colleges providing remedial, standard, and advanced courses in, 17; percentage of total curriculum in, 23; total student enrollment figures for, 47
Course levels, relationship between liberal arts, transfer rates, and, 81–91
Cureton, J., 15, 63, 64

Daniels, R., 59
Desruisseaux, P., 55

Education, 21; number of sections and percentage of courses offered, 22; percentage of total curriculum in, 23
Eells, W. C., 81
El Paso Community College, English as a Second Language at, 49, 57, 58, 59
Engineering technologies, 20–21; number of sections and percentage of courses offered, 22; percentage of total curriculum in, 23

English, 15, 33–34; enrollment and average class size in, 16; percentage of colleges offering liberal arts classes in, by institutional size, 19; percentage of colleges providing remedial, standard, and advanced courses in, 17; percentage of total curriculum in, 23; total student enrollment figures for, 47

English as a Second Language (ESL), 15, 35, 49, 90, 97, 104; community college population, 56–58; enrollment projections, 58–59; implications for policy and planning, 59–61; national statistics on limited English proficient adults, immigrants, refugees, and foreign students and, 51–56; results of 1991 National Curriculum Study and, 50–51

Ethnic studies, 63–66; enrollment in, 66–67; size of college and, 67–68; suggestions for future research related to, 69

Fine and performing arts, 34; enrollment and average class size in, 16; percentage of colleges offering liberal arts classes in, by institutional size, 19; percentage of colleges providing remedial, standard, and advanced courses in, 17 percentage of total curriculum in, 23; total student enrollment figures for, 47

Ford Foundation, 73, 74

Foreign languages, 15

Foreign students, English as a Second Language and, 51, 55–56

Frank, K. A., 94

Garcia, P., 76

General education: graduation requirements, 43–48; liberal arts versus, 32

General Education in a Free Society, 32

Gleazer, E., 8

Graduation requirements general education, 43–48; liberal arts, 43–48

Greenfield, R. K., 83

Grubb, N., 18, 94

Harry S. Truman College, English as a Second Language at, 49, 57, 58

Health, 20; number of sections and percentage of courses offered, 22; percentage of total curriculum in, 23

Herzberg, G., 32

Hispanic Americans, 64, 102

History, 15

Home economics, 20; number of sections and percentage of courses offered, 22; percentage of total curriculum in, 23

Hull, D., 8

Humanities, 34–35; enrollment and average class size in, 16; percentage of colleges offering liberal arts classes in, by institutional size, 19; percentage of colleges providing remedial, standard, and advanced courses in, 17; percentage of total curriculum, 23; total student enrollment figures for, 47

Hunter, R., 77

Huss, S., 54, 55

Illinois Community College Board, 27

Illinois State University, 27, 28

Immigrants, English as a Second Language and, 51, 53–55

Immigration Reform and Control Act (IRCA), 53, 54, 55, 58

Institute of International Education (IIE), 55

Karabel, J., 8, 93

Kintzer, F. C., 82

Knoell, D. M., 82

Koos, L. V., 81

Krogh, L. C., 38

Latinos, 63

Lee, V. E., 94

Lee College, 26

Levine, A., 15, 63, 64

Lewis, L. L., 44, 46

Liberal arts, 13, 14–18, 31; choosing a curriculum in, 33; general education versus, 32; graduation requirements, 43–48; ratio of non–liberal arts to, 22–23; relationship between course levels, transfer rates, and, 81–91; total student enrollment figures for, 47

Limited English proficient (LEP) adults: English as a Second Language and, 51, 52–53

Linguistic isolation, 52, 53

Literature, 15

Lombardi, J., 82

McGrath, D., 83

Mainstreaming, 84

Marketing and distribution, 20; number of sections and percentage of courses offered, 22; percentage of total curriculum in, 23

Martorana, S. V., 60

Mathematics, 15, 36–37; enrollment and average class size in, 16; percentage of colleges offering liberal arts classes in, by institutional size, 19; percentage of colleges providing remedial, standard, and advanced courses in, 17; percentage of total curriculum in, 23; total student enrollment figures for, 47

Mexican Americans, 64–65

Miami–Dade Community College, 57, 58

Minorities in Higher Education, 93

Minority students, 93–96; nonwhite students and curriculum, 96–98; nonwhite students and transfer, 98–100

National Curriculum Study (1991), 46, 49, 57, 65, 94; English as a Second Language and, 50–51, 56–62

National Endowment for the Humanities, 13

National Liberal Arts Curriculum Study, 22

National Science Board, 38

Native Americans, 63, 64

Nelson, S., 93

Non–liberal arts, 18, 20–21; agriculture technology, 20, 22; amount of curriculum occupied by, 21–22; business and office, 20, 22; education, 21, 22; engineering technologies, 20–21, 22; health, 20, 22; home economics, 20, 22; marketing and distribution, 20, 22; methodology of, 18, 20; personal skills and avocational courses, 21, 22; ratio of liberal arts to, 22–23; technical education, 20; trade and industry, 21, 22; transferability rates and, 23–24

Orfield, G., 71, 101

Ottinger, C. A., 44

Parnell, D., 8

Pasadena City College, English as a Second Language at, 50, 57, 58

Passaic County Community College, English as a Second Language at, 49, 57

Paul, F. G., 71, 101

Personal skills, 21 number of sections and percentage of courses offered, 22; percentage of total curriculum in, 23

Peterson, A., 64

Physics, 15

Pincus, F., 93, 94

Political science, 15

Portés, A., 53

Raisman, N., 44

Refugees, English as a Second Language and, 51, 53–55

Remedial courses, 14, 15; percentage of colleges providing, 17

"Requirements in Undergraduate General Education," 44

Richardson, R., 18, 93

Rudolph, F., 32, 36, 37

Rumbaut, R. G., 53

Saeed, A. M., 58

Santa Monica College, foreign students at, 55

Sciences, 37–38; enrollment and average class size in, 16; percentage of colleges offering liberal arts classes in, by institutional size, 19; percentage of colleges providing remedial, standard, and advanced courses in, 17; percentage of total curriculum in, 23; total student enrollment figures for, 47

Scott-Skillman, T., 58

Sheldon, M. S., 77

Social sciences, 38–40; percentage of colleges offering liberal arts classes in, by institutional size, 19; percentage of total curriculum in, 23; total student enrollment figures for, 47

Sophomore curriculum, 84–85

Southwest Texas, 25

Spear, M. B., 83

Standard courses, 14; percentage of colleges providing, 17

Statistical Yearbook of the Immigration and Naturalization Service, 53

Stephen F. Austin State, 25

Takahata, G., 79

"Taxonomy of Academic and Vocational Courses for Less-than-4-Year Postsecondary Institutions," 18

Technical education, 20; number of sections and percentage of courses offered, 22; percentage of total curriculum in, 23

Texas Tech, 26

Tracking, 84

Trade and industry, 21; number of sections and percentage of courses offered, 22; percentage of total curriculum in, 23

Transfer Assembly project, 71, 73–75, 77, 78, 85, 94, 97

Transfer rates, 71–72, 75–79; definition of, 72–73; disparities related to, 102–103; factors affecting, 82–83; future and, 103–105; minority students and, 98–100; national, 75; of non–liberal arts, 23–28; relationship between liberal arts, course levels, and, 81–91; Transfer Assembly methodology and, 73–75

Triton, 97

Turner, E., 54

University of California (UC) system, 24, 25, 28

University of Houston–Main, 26

University of Illinois at Urbana-Champaign, 27, 28

University of Texas at Austin, 25

Vocational education, 94, 97

Watkins, B. T., 55, 83

Williamsburg Technical College, 97

Yuba College, 57

Zemsky, R., 33

Zikopoulos, M., 55

ORDERING INFORMATION

NEW DIRECTIONS FOR COMMUNITY COLLEGES is a series of paperback books that provides expert assistance to help community colleges meet the challenges of their distinctive and expanding educational mission. Books in the series are published quarterly in Spring, Summer, Fall, and Winter and are available for purchase by subscription and individually.

SUBSCRIPTIONS for 1994 cost $49.00 for individuals (a savings of 25 percent over single-copy prices) and $72.00 for institutions, agencies, and libraries. Please do not send institutional checks for personal subscriptions. Standing orders are accepted.

SINGLE COPIES cost $16.95 when payment accompanies order. (California, New Jersey, New York, and Washington, D.C., residents please include appropriate sales tax.) All orders will be charged postage and handling.

DISCOUNTS FOR QUANTITY ORDERS are available. Please write to the address below for information.

ALL ORDERS must include either the name of an individual or an official purchase order number. Please submit your order as follows:
Subscriptions: specify series and year subscription is to begin
Single copies: include individual title code (such as CC82)

MAIL ALL ORDERS TO:
Jossey-Bass Publishers
350 Sansome Street
San Francisco, California 94104-1342

FOR SUBSCRIPTION SALES OUTSIDE OF THE UNITED STATES, contact any international subscription agency or Jossey-Bass directly.